VEGGIE
LONDON

by
Craig John Wilson

Photographs by Chris Windsor

VEGGIE LONDON

Written by Craig John Wilson
Photography by Chris Windsor
Cover Photography by Colin Hawkins
Edited by Abigail Willis
Design by Susi Koch

Published in 1997 by
Metro Publications
PO Box 6336
London
N1 6PY

Printed in Great Britain by:
The Burlington Press
Foxton
Cambridge

British Library Cataloguing in
Publication Data.
A catalogue record for this book is
available from the British Library.
ISBN 09522914 1 X

To Selina for her continuous inspiration and encouragement.

ACKNOWLEDGEMENTS

With Special Thanks to:

Rosie Kindersley
Nick Walker
Brixton Brady

Eating partners:

Dawn Amos
Lisa Baker
Tom Heatherwick
Liza Monks
Simon Murphy
Malin Palm
Peter Snow
Diane Torr
Russell Webley
Lindy Wiffen
Nancy Wilden

Thanks also to those who have offered tips, useful information, and sound advice:

Deborah Anderson
Celia Brooks-Brown
Nick Buglione
Al Hoff
Andrew Kershman
Jennifer Joyce
Suzie Patel
Sophie Mathias
Paul and Tori Schumacher at Earthquake Produce

CONTENTS

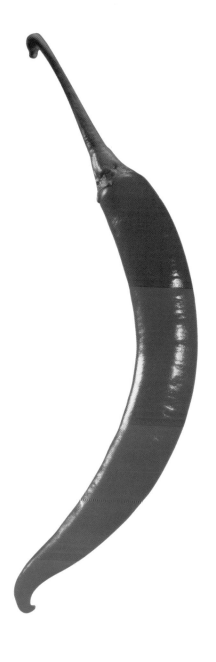

About the author

Craig John Wilson has been a vegetarian (on and off) for seventeen years. He has written on sport for Socialist Youth, Leyton Orientear, The Guardian, and ES Magazine. Veggie London is his first book on food. He lives in South London with his wife, painter and cook Selina Snow.

INTRODUCTION

There are many reasons why people give up eating meat. Religious or political, ethical or economic, for health reasons or as the result of food scares, and sometimes simply because some dislike the taste or texture of animal flesh. The Vegetarian Society estimate that 72% of Londoners believe there will be less meat eating in future.

A whole subculture has grown up around vegetarianism – one thinks of vegetarian cafes or wholefood stores as being bastions of the tie-dye t-shirt, aromatherapy oil, and relaxation tapes. While conceding that the 'new age' movement has contributed much to the debates about cruelty free living, I have attempted to take a new approach to the subject. It makes little difference to me why you should want to eat vegetarian food, but I hope that when you do, it should be of a high quality, well-served and presented, and with a love for the ingredients. For if there's one problem I've found in my research, it's not that cooks don't love animals, it's that they don't love vegetables.

In researching this book, I felt rather like Raymond Postgate, that post-war foodie hero, who almost single-handedly (with his Good Food Guides), raised British food out of the boiled beef and steamed pudding era. For there are many vegetarian restaurants, that get by with sloppy (and sometimes downright rude) service, with poor ingredients, and certainly with badly cooked second rate food. Vegetarians need their food to be simply and quickly cooked, in order to retain both flavour and nutritional value. Vegetables are, on the whole delicate, and need to be treated with love. Many long standing veggie restaurants don't seem to understand this, and perhaps this is why so many have closed in the past two years.

Coming to the rescue have been, perhaps surprisingly (and somewhat sacrilegiously) many of London's meaty restaurants. There are several reasons for this. With so many Londoners becoming vegetarian or at least cutting down on their meat intake (what Lanesborough Chef Paul Gayler calls 'virtually vegetarian'), restaurants have decided, for good economic reasons, to cater to that section of their clientele. Restaurants have in any case started to soak up the best methods and ingredients of Thai, Indian, Chinese and Mediterranean food - with their unparalleled freshness, flavour, and aroma – influences that have led to what the Australian food guru, Jill Dupleix, calls 'The New Food'.

Lastly Britain has been indebted (as it has for much of it's post-war rebuilding) to the influences of new Londoners – those restauranteurs from East Africa, South East Asia, the Caribbean, the Med., and the Middle-East. These established cuisines respect vegetables, and unlike us meat and two veg Brits, do not relegate the vegetable to second class status and a choice of potatoes or peas. The best restaurants, both veggie and non, are cooking foods with flavours from outside the UK.

You can use Veggie London in several ways. Restaurants are listed first of all geographically. Work out where you are, where you want to eat, and away you go. I have listed rail or tube stations, but have decided that with privatisation, bus routes are sadly highly variable and short lived. Secondly, once you've decided what kind of food you want to eat, you'll find a list of restaurants at the back of the book indicating the nationality of the food each serves, you can then refer to the review in the main section. Thirdly, I have included a rough pricing guide. Although vegetarian food is nearly always the food of the poor (in India or Isleworth, relatively speaking), you'll still want to budget. The prices are for a main meal and dessert without wine or beer.

£ Under £5
££ £5-10
£££ £10-15
££££ £15-20
£££££ £20 and upwards

Londoners – hungry, hardworking, and frequently hassled – have a wide choice of vegetarian eating places to choose from. While Vegetarian London reviews many traditional veggie restaurants however, it also looks at the options for eating meat-free meals in London's wonderful array of Ethnic restaurants.

I should mention my restaurant prejudices - iceberg lettuce, bad service, and loud music. You'll have your own, but one thing we all agree on is that we want food of a higher standard, and more information about what we're eating. My advice is to ask and keep asking. We must all the keep up the pressure on restaurants to start giving us the sort of vegetarian choice, and the information about what we're buying, that the high street food stores have given us.

ETHNIC FOOD

AFRICAN & CARIBBEAN

Despite four hundred years of diaspora, the foods of West African, the Caribbean and Black Britain share as many similarities as differences. Much of this is due to the three way trade in slaves, sugar and manufactured goods that continued until the mid part of the last century, which carried with it new foods and ways of cooking. Yam, plantain and groundnuts are eaten in both Africa and the Caribbean, yet the groundnut is a native of Brazil. Cassava and maize were introduced to Africa from North America, while coffee and millet travelled in the other direction. The shores of West Africa and the fertile islands of the Caribbean were quite literally 'hothouses' for the plants introduced there.

There are exotic inspirations in the style of cooking too, and particularly in the spicing. The cuisines of the indigenous peoples, and those of their colonial European conquerors, were supplemented by flavours from further afield. Eastern and Southern Africa soaked up influences from India and Malaya. In Trinidad too cooking betrays an Indian flavour, as the British brought with them Indian workers to administrate the colony.

There have been Black Britons since Roman times, but it was the savagery of the slave trade which first bought large numbers of Africans to London. In this century, Africans and Caribbeans came to London to serve the Empire during both World Wars and were a crucial factor in the building of Britain's short-lived but highly successful Welfare State. The National Health Service, London Transport and British Rail all recruited directly from the Islands.

Immigrants settled in what were, at the time, the poorer areas of London. Trinidadians established a community in Notting Hill, starting (and still taking the lead in) the famous Carnival. Brixton was a Jamaican area, and became the focal point for black life and resistance in Britain, though some say Dalston is now the hub of Black life. Many Ghanaians settled in Balham and Tooting, Kenyans in Edgware and Kingsbury, and there is a large Zairean community on the Mile End Road. Although immigration from the Caribbean slowed down in the 1970s, it continued from Kenya and Ghana and in the last few years there has been a steady trickle of refugees from Somalia and Ethiopia as the civil war continues.

African and Caribbean foods are prepared and eaten in a relaxed, no-nonsense manner and they are rarely eaten formally, but instead are enjoyed over conversation and music, with friends and family. Perhaps this is why some African and Caribbean restaurants in Britain have a reputation for inconsistent standards. Things are changing however.

The vegetarian is normally well served in an Afro-Caribbean restaurant; many of London's restaurants serve foods from both continents, and often feature Cajun or Creole food as well. The staples – rice and peas, cassava, okra, yam and dasheen, groundnut – are delicious and, with the addition of chillies, nutmeg, coconut milk, plantain or banana, the gifted Afro-Caribbean cook can improvise a palate that tastes like nothing else, transcending its myriad influences. That is the genius of African and Caribbean cooking.

ETHNIC FOOD

CENTRAL AMERICA

When, at the invitation of Montezuma, the Spanish Conquistadors first rode into Tenochtitlan (now Mexico City), they found a civilised city the size of Constantinople with networks of government and communication, and a religion and culture perhaps older than their own. It was a city with an established cuisine of exotic and wonderful foodstuffs. As historian Jonathan Norton Leonard observes, "The Spanish, obsessed by gold, did not at first realise that the real treasure of the Americas was sweet corn, potatoes, tomatoes, chillies, chocolate, tobacco, avocados, peanuts, cassava (manioc or yucca), beans, vanilla, sweet potatoes, pineapples and papayas."

The food of the civilised Indian cultures of South America, in particular potatoes and corn, have since become the staple crops of 50% of the world's population. Amazing when you consider that there may have only been 12 million Indians. Agriculture was highly advanced however and in corn the Indians had a crop that could survive and thrive in almost infinite variations of climate and environment. Spanish may be a common language but Central America is extremely diverse both geographically and culturally taking in desert and rain forest, mountains, and an extensive coastline.

The Indians not only grew corn, which in itself lacks nutritional value (though much of the world's animal produce is created by livestock fed on it), but had discovered that combining it with beans aided vitamin absorption, and that when planted together each assisted the growth and survival of the other. They were also a delicious flavour combination.

There is also the matter of the chilli. There are probably as many types of chilli as there are corn but outside the countries where they're grown, you'll find a poor choice. My friend Paul Schumacher of Earthquake Produce in California is a chilli connoisseur and eats the things raw. He claims they contain more vitamin C than an orange, stave off colds and flu, discourage mosquitoes, are antibacterial, thin the blood and aid digestion. More than that, they add a kick to most meals that becomes addictive, and can bring out the flavour of anything from a potato to an egg.

While spuds and sweet corn made their way to Europe to spark off the barbecue and fast food revolutions, the invading colonials – mostly Spanish, but also large numbers of English, Germans, Italians and Dutch – recreated their own cuisines using local ingredients. The Spanish had an advanced and well entrenched food culture, with a heavy Moorish influence, and introduced not only sugar cane, lemon, and pork to the New World, but also their spices and love of thick sauces. Slaves from West Africa brought expertise and produce unavailable in Europe, but the heart of Latin American food remains South American Indian.

This is particularly true of Mexico. The majority of London's Latin American restaurants are Mexican, or Tex-Mex (American with Mexican influences) and most 'International' menus will feature some combination of burritos, tacos, or fajitas and chilli. As it happens, few are truly owned or run by Mexicans, and while this may not always be a problem (the best take-away veggie burritos in the world, at Bueno Bueno outside San Francisco, are made by a Finn!), it is in London. Not enough attention is paid to the food, too much to the garish gas station tat on the walls. Many are fun theme restaurants and can be enjoyed as such, but it's a shame, for Mexican food has much to offer the veggie bon viveur.

While the Spanish introduced the pig to the Americas, and therefore pork-fat for frying rice or flavouring, meat is not essential to Latin food. Bread is a basic – and as corn is without gluten (which binds air into the dough) it is flat and malleable – ideal for wrapping your food in, or perhaps for using as a plate. And there is a world of American produce to plop on top of it or serve it with – in various delicious combinations there are tomatoes, chillies, avocado, coriander, lime, pineapple, squash, papaya, and of course beans. This is a food perhaps best eaten at home while we await the arrival of decent Mexican dining experiences.

ETHNIC FOOD

BRITISH

"It's official" announced Time Out a couple of years ago, "British food is fashionable". Bad news for vegetarians I'm afraid, for the New British restaurants, the Chop Houses and French Houses, have hardly made the vegetarian a priority. This is not surprising, for Britain, with its temperate climate, has no great culture of vegetarianism. Animal life, both cultivated and wild, has been abundant since prehistoric times, and although the existence of mincemeat (the sort in Christmas mince pies) is evidence of shortage or absence of meat (which it was invented to stretch out or replace), and although British cuisine was built on a foundation of disguising poor quality meat, no great culinary art evolved to aid doing without it (as in China or India).

The British instead perfected the art of roasting, and characteristics of our cuisine are still substantiality, comfort, fullness. It is uncomplicated, reassuring, and best cooked at home (many of my friends cook a fine veggie roast but none of the restaurants do). We cook to keep out the cold and to fill the stomach with warmth, for although we do not have a climate as such, we certainly have weather. Vegetables do not stand up well to traditional British cooking styles, and tend to lose both flavour and nutrition.

British vegetarians have had a hard time of it. The great socialist writer George Orwell, surely a liberal thinker, loathed vegetarians and described them as "sandal-wearers", lumping them with naturists and pacifists in his personal pantheon of weirdos and eccentrics. During World War II vegetarians fought a long, hard battle with the Ministry of Food to swap their meat coupons for cheese and other products, and Lord Woolton told them he had "worried a great deal about the vegetarians, and sometimes laid awake at night thinking about them". Even Cranks, that great proselytizer of vegetarian lifestyle, has named itself somewhat mockingly.

So Britain has yet to develop a convincing and unique response to vegetarian tastes, though ironically there are more vegetarian restaurants in London than in any other European city. It's just that the food in those establishments is more likely to be influenced by Indian, Thai or Chinese cuisines.

CHINESE

I t may seem ridiculously obvious, but there are an awful lot of Chinese in China. In fact there are 1088 million of them and though the country is the size of Europe, and situated between comparable latitudes with similar weather patterns, it is very mountainous. Ninety per cent of the European landmass is available for farming, but China has only eleven per cent on which to feed its people. The Chinese therefore put the emphasis on growing efficient food crops rather than livestock which takes up scant land and resources. Chinese protein comes predominantly from wheat, rice, gluten and the ubiquitous soya bean.

With such a huge population, life is hard and eating has become a major pre-occupation. As one of the world's oldest continuous civilizations, the Chinese have had several millennia to develop a cuisine which makes the most of sometimes minimal ingredients. It is not for nothing that food is referred to in the abstract as "rice".

Chinese food, as with much of the culture, is about balance. The highly structured formal meal should have contrast in flavour, texture, aroma and presentation. Highly spiced foods will be offset by banal dishes. On a similar note, all dishes are accorded respect at the table and no one course predominates (as the Sunday joint might at home).

Although meat has often been scarce for the Chinese, a vegetarian tradition has survived largely due to devout Buddhists and monks. They have developed a cuisine which simulates meat, but is made of fungus, egg protein, or soya. Unfortunately this kind of food is hard to find in Britain and even within China is a minority taste. Like many people, the Chinese equate vegetarianism with poverty.

Very few dairy products are used as the Chinese are lactose intolerant, but one should be careful when eating vegetarian dishes as stock is often made from beef or chicken. Chinese cuisine however has much to offer the vegetarian. The quick cooking times and high temperatures in the wok, for instance, seal in vitamins, preserve flavours and excite the palate. Traditional Chinese meal combinations of mushrooms, grains, and vegetables can help with the absorption of proteins and minerals.

There are four distinct schools within Chinese cuisine, but the vast majority of London's restaurants (and indeed throughout the western world) are Cantonese. This is because the Cantonese were the earliest to migrate in numbers. Canton is a region abundant in natural resources, and it is said that its chefs are the finest in China. The food is subtle, lacking extremes. Oil is used sparingly, though cooks are skilled in the use of the wok, and they are particularly fond of nuts and fungi. By contrast, the food of Sichuan and Hunan uses generous amounts of chilli, which acts as both a preservative and, in the humid climate, a natural air conditioner. In the area around Shanghai, fish and seafood are popular, though vegetarians can also delight in delicacies cooked with soy sauce and sugar. Food is often salty and stews and rich sauces are common. In Northern China, wheat is more common than rice and the basic starches are supplied by noodles, thin pancakes and steamed dumplings, often seasoned with garlic, onion, or leeks.

9

EASTERN EUROPEAN & JEWISH

I f Westerners talk of Eastern Europe as a single entity, it is a consequence of the Cold War. The Czech Republic is further north and west than Austria, and before the World War II was the seventh wealthiest nation on earth. Poland is a country with an almost unbroken national culture of Catholicism despite conquest and partition by Sweden, Russia and Germany. Russia, even in it's post-Glasnost state, is a huge country, crossing time zones and climates.

It is the food of Russia, the Czech regions of Moravia and Bohemia, and particularly of Poland, that we find most often on the streets of London. A century or more of political unrest have seen steady trickles of educated, skilled migrants who come to London to escape from persecution or destitution.

Despite the cultural differences, the food of these Slavic neighbours is very similar. Much of this is to do with climate. It is bitterly cold and winter is a long and unforgiving season. Root crops, laying protected beneath the earth, survive better than tree fruits. Potatoes, carrots, turnips and beetroots form the basis of most diets. Bread is made from hardier, more dependable grains such as rye, and in summer there are abundant berries and apples. Meat however, is still a major part of the diet, even though of poor quality and expensive to buy.

Vegans are particularly hard done by, for Russians, Poles and Czechs love sour cream, butter, cheeses and yoghurt (Czech yoghurt is wonderful). While people in the east enjoy fresh vegetables, they are not easy to come by. Pickling, traditionally a way of preserving both flavour and nutrients through winter, is a must. Jams, preserves and compotes are also popular. Russians and Poles are partial to mushrooms, abundant in the forests, and they're as fond of a morel as a Frenchman is of a truffle. Unfortunately these rarely make it to London restaurants. Slavic staples are soup, kasha (a bulgar-like cracked grain) and bread, none of which need contain meat but such pride is taken in hearty meat dishes that you will do well to find one without in London or Gdansk.

Restaurants from these countries do not have a good reputation, but things are changing with an increasing number of Georgian and Ukrainian restaurants opening up. They will hopefully be more skilled in the culinary arts than their predecessors, and it will be interesting to see where they take the cooking of the east.

A safer bet for veggies, and one with many similarities to Slavic food, is Jewish cuisine, particularly as Britain's Jewish community is predominantly Ashkenazic (of Eastern European origin) as opposed to Sephardic or Spanish. Jewish dishes have been a great influence on the cooking of Poland, for in the fourteenth century King Casimir fell in love with the beautiful Jewish princess Esterka and because of their love Poland became a sanctuary for the tyrannized European Jewry. The word 'nosh' is a Yiddish word taken from the German 'naschen' to chew – presumably the word 'gnashers' (as in teeth) shares the same root.

Jewish dietary law (kashrut) is complex and governs dietary choice, food preparation, cooking and eating. For instance meat and diary products must be kept apart, even to the extent of eating them at separate meals. As all work (even cooking) is forbidden on the Sabbath, food must be prepared in advance and Jewish cooks have developed many cold dishes for eating on the Shabbat. There is also an extensive range of dairy dishes, 'pareve', which contain neither meat nor milk (there is even pareve ice-cream!).

It is a shame that the tradition of dairy restaurants never caught on in London as it did in New York. They even exist in Poland. In these one can eat glorious meat free dishes - blintzes, borscht, latkes, piroshki - and taste the tradition of centuries. You will find these dishes on the menu of many Jewish restaurants and delis but, unfortunately for vegetarians, you may well have to watch the salt-beef being cut in the window.

FRENCH

ETHNIC FOOD

For the last few summers Selina and I have driven through France to stay at a small village in Provence. It hasn't quite been ruined by the English, despite our presence and the Peter Mayle effect. I guess he was right about one thing though – the food – for Provence boasts some of the freshest and most delicious vegetables I've ever eaten. Every evening we settled down to plump olives, fruity tomatoes, oily avocados, or tangy bell peppers. The fruit is alive with flavour, the wine and olive oil both good enough to drink.

Coming back to some of the restaurants I've featured in this book was positively depressing after the treasures on offer in Provence (although there are around 30 regions in France, each with its own cuisine and ethnic identity, Provençale food is probably the best for veggies).

France is big, twice the size of Britain but with a comparable population and, as those drives taught us, it's geographically diverse. Mountains, plains, dense forests and deeply agricultural. All that space makes the French hungry and they appreciate fine food in ways that the English can only wonder at. A small French grocery shop or the daily market is a wonder of seasonal local produce, bursting with vitamins and flavour. The strength of French cooking is that it makes the most of these ingredients.

There are generally accepted to be two types of French cooking, the 'classical' (so called 'haute cuisine'), and the 'provincial'. Classic French cuisine is a rarefied world of expensive ingredients cooked to precise and demanding rules. It is an art form, taught like classical music, and requiring an appreciation of the works of maestros throughout the ages who have taken the methods one step further to create their masterpieces. The west derives its culinary language from French and its greatest chefs and restaurants are normally French. It has held an influence over the cooking of the western world that is perhaps out of all proportion to its content. As the food writer MFK Fisher once said "[Classical] French cooking can mean mediocre or poor or dishonest cooking, served with pomp in pretentious restaurants everywhere."

Some would argue that classically trained chefs are always the best, and essential in raising the standards of other cuisines. The Proof of the pudding is in the eating, and those who have stuffed themselves with provincial French cooking, the food of the everyday French bistro, know that cheaper and quicker is not always poorer.

French cooking is heavy on the meat. The list of famous French vegetarians is thin, the likelihood of finding a vegetarian restaurant even thinner. Vegans can more or less forget it. This isn't such a problem in London, where French restaurants are either extremely expensive, or fall into Fisher's pomp/pretentious category. But generally it's a shame. The French have a way with the simplest ingredients - potatoes, a few fresh herbs, an omelette and a glass of wine (as Elizabeth David once said), that allow vegetables to be wonders in their own right. Read Edouard De Pomaine's unaffected recipes for omelettes or scrambled eggs for mouth watering non-meat meals that anyone can master. Except, it seems, French restaurant owners putting together menus for vegetarians in London – they just can't resist complicating the issue.

INDIAN

The Indian subcontinent is vast, stretching 2000 miles from north to south and east to west. Home of the some of the world's most ancient civilizations, one thousand million people live and work there, the vast majority vegetarians. Although this is partly a result of economic circumstances, it is also due to religious belief. Hindus, Buddhists and Jains all ascribe to the principle of ahimsa – nonviolence and respect for life. Jains, for instance, live predominantly on rice, pulses and leaves, so as to avoid killing earth dwelling creatures such as worms and insects. Others shun eggs and even tomatoes, blood-red fruits and vegetables.

Such a huge landmass varies greatly in climate. From the Himalayas in the north, through plain, desert and jungle, the land is as varied is its people – a polyglot mix of cultures, religions and invaders, all of whom, over thousands of years, have made their impact on the food of the region.

The civilizations of the Middle East, and later Europe, came to trade spices, which were abundant in India and valued for medicinal as well as ceremonial and culinary purposes. All of these influences – religious, geographical, historical – have come to bear on what many consider the most exciting food in the world.

Even the smallest village in Britain has an Indian take-away. It is almost the only dining out certainty we have and London is nothing if not a collection of villages. It should therefore come as no surprise that there are over 1200 Indian restaurants in London. Although most of these restaurants offer a vegetable biryani, and are generally reliable stand-bys for veggies, it is unfortunate that many of these restaurants are unimaginative, of poor quality: and that 85% of them are owned by Bangladeshis who, being mainly Moslem, are meat eaters. Not that you'll find authentic Bangladeshi cuisine even then - Bangladesh is a vast delta plain, draining the rivers of the Ganges and the Brahmaputra, and Bangladeshis eat a lot of rice and fish. Most Indian restaurants cater to British tastes - mutton and chicken are fairly common items onn the menu .

The vegetarian in need of a regular curry fix should head for a South Indian or Gujurati cafe. Both regions are predominantly Hindu and avoid meat: the majority of Indian restaurants I have listed fall into these categories. South Indian food is spicy and full of tang; coconut and mustard oil are used to prepare light, quick snacks – bhel poori or dosa – many of which are sold from huts and stalls on Bombay streets.

Gujurat is a Hindu state situated in the dry North-west and its cuisine features breads rather than rice (which needs plenty of water). The food is simple, making use of wheat, yoghurt and subtle spicing. It is often sweeter (some say blander) than the food of other regions.Northern Indian food, on the other hand has absorbed influences from its trading partners over the centuries, from Afghanistan, Kurdistan and as far away as Persia. The clay tandoori oven is used and the creamy food served with bread, though rice is always on London menus.

There has been a recent trend in London for the Balti, as much an import from Birmingham's Pakistani community as from Pakistan itself. A balti (also called a 'karahi') is an iron wok used in parts of Pakistan, and freshly cooked food is eaten straight from the pan with bread. In London this may well mean bog-standard curry slung into a balti before serving, so beware. Good balti houses look like fast food cafés - formica tables, quick service, cheap food and Sunrise Radio. If it looks too much like a restaurant it's probably not authentic.

Geographically the Brick Lane area is Bangladeshi while Southall and Whitechapel are good for food from Pakistan and the Punjab. Wembley, Kilburn and Hampstead have many South Indian eateries.

ITALIAN

Young vegetarians could never have survived the past twenty or thirty years without Italian food, for what student, veggie or not, hasn't survived on a diet of pizza, pasta and coffee? It is fortunate remarked Elizabeth David, that the Italians are not great meat eaters, for they have given world cuisine a huge legacy of mouthwatering meatless dishes. Even the most traditional Italian meal, which is structured around six courses, has only one meat dish and as Italians rarely serve vegetables and meat on the same course, it is easy for the vegetarian to miss that one out and still enjoy a varied and exciting meal.

Actually it is slightly misleading to even think of Italian food. The Eskimo has around fifty different words for snow but no generic term, and Italians talk about food in the same way. It has only been a century and a half since the unification of the separate Italian states. Each region was alive with a history, language and culture very much its own, and often in bitter rivalry with its neighbours. There is still a sense of this on the menu – dishes proudly proclaim themselves Genovese, Fiorentina, Neapolitan, and Veneziana.

The Romans, as with much besides, took advice from the Greeks on cooking, but with the fall of Rome the traditions were lost, only to be resurrected during the great renaissance of the fifteenth century. The spice trade was also nfluential (as it was throughout the Mediterranean), and cities such as Venice grew rich on import taxes. However, the Italian food we know and enjoy owes less to the powerful families of Florence and Genoa than to the hard-working peasant communities of the twenty-one regions of the country who ate simple fresh food, cooked without curlicues or extravagance. Italian food, like the Italians themselves, is approachable and congenial.

What the Londoner knows of Italian food seems mostly to be confined to pizza and pasta, and although there are many splendid little cafes serving those filling staples (particularly in Soho, which Italian immigrants have done much to shape over the past 100 years), they should not miss out on regional variations and delicacies. In the industrial north - Milan, Bologna, Genoa – where, as in Britain, agriculture is highly mechanised, food is often rich with egg, cheese, butter and mushrooms. Sage and rosemary tantalise the tongue. In the south, where much of the land is still worked by small scale peasant farmers, foods still echo those of Greece – olive oil instead of butter, fresh vegetables, sheep and goat cheeses. Pasta (said to have been introduced from China by Marco Polo) is a staple of the south and although popular all over Italy, Northerners also enjoy rice, and in Lombardy and the Veneto, polenta, a porridge like substance made from yellow maize.

It is never a problem finding vegetarian courses at Italian restaurants, so vegetarians should try and seek out the best. Italians came in their hundreds of thousands to Britain, poverty and political unrest creating a great diaspora, matched only in Europe by the Irish. And like the Irish (who physically built the infrastructure of the country) they have brought much, (continuing to influence our culinary traditions – as any visit to a supermarket pasta section, or meal in a 'Modern British' restaurant proves). Vegetarians have much to thank Italian cooks for and would do well to study their methods of creating simple, wholesome meatless meals.

JAPANESE

Japan is a country with more than its fair share of mountains, and what isn't mountainous is covered in thick forest. Very little land is available for cultivation, but what there is is carefully farmed to get the most from meagre resources. It's no surprise then that the Japanese are not great meat eaters (raising animals for food is an ineffective use of land).

A nation of islanders, the Japanese have always eaten fish and vegetables are also an important part of the diet. It is rice however that is the staple of Japan. The Japanese word Gohan means both 'rice' and 'meal'. Other foods are called okazu, which can be translated as 'subsidiary foods', and rice is eaten in many ways: as a grain, as noodles, or drunk as sake – rice wine. Japanese cooking, like the culture, developed a distinctive style through political and geographical isolation. Although there was a period of Chinese influence between the sixth and eighth centuries, it wasn't until the Portugese came to trade in the seventeenth century that the country was opened up to outside influence. The cuisine is highly refined, and as Jenny Linford, author of Food Lovers' London, notes, "is both aesthetic and ascetic". Under the ethical influence of Zen, food is treated with great respect, both in its preparation and its presentation. Food should be fresh, with the emphasis on bringing out the natural flavour of the ingredients. Flavours are limited to salt, sweet and sour, but are often combined to enhance the food. Soy sauce, sake and dashi (a stock made from seaweed) are flavour bases for Japanese dishes, and a meal should be balanced both in terms of ingredients and presentation. Japanese cooking is neither a cheap, nor a particularly quick option, especially if done properly, for great attention is placed on good ingredients, on texture, colour and shape, and it is demanding on the chef.

Zen Buddhism, the tenets of which have permeated every aspect of Japanese society, insists on the sanctity of life and respect for one's fellow beings. Because Japan is also geographically unsuitable for beef or lamb, the Japanese eat vegetables without reservation and even though they enjoy seafood and fish, the vegetable is never a side dish to meat. That the Japanese have developed a taste for beef in the post-War years is a reflection of their love affair with all things American.

In Japan restaurants tend to specialise in one or another style of cooking - noodle bars for instance - but in Britain they will offer a selection from a variety of styles. They developed mostly as a response to the growing numbers of Japanese businessmen in London. The post-War economic miracle has brought thousands of Japanese families to London on short term business contracts and, over the past few years, tens of thousands of Japanese students. There are increasing numbers of Japanese stores in London too, not only in Soho, or in Finchley, but most notably in the vast Japanese mega-complex that is Yaohan Plaza in Colindale, home to Abeno (see page 38).

To prepare and present food in the Japanese manner is hard to do well (and therefore cheaply) without years of training, and it is likely to be some time before its distinctive flavours and textures become commonplace on British streets. But restaurants like Wagamama, adding western presentation to Japanese tradition, are doing much to popularise the cuisine, which can only be good news for vegetarians.

MIDDLE EASTERN

You might imagine it was difficult to treat the Middle East as a single entity for this book. After all, the area ranges for one and a half million square miles - from Greece in the west, to Iran in the east, and north to south from Turkey to Egypt. 232 million people live in the region, "speaking five major languages, writing in four alphabets, and professing three of the world's great religions" as Time Life magazine succinctly put it.

But the history of the area, prey to invasion and counter invasion, over roads that were major trade routes between west and east, has meant that this is not quite so ridiculous after all. The Persian, Greek, Roman, Byzantine and Ottoman empires all laid claim to the area, and despite the large Christian and Jewish populations, Islam is a uniting force.

It was in the Middle East, in what we now know as Iraq, that mankind first cultivated the soil and raised cattle. The area was rich in milk, honey and spices and its popular image in the west - of desertification and drought - is both recent and misleading.

The area is abundant in vegetables and fruits, legumes and grains all of which have found their way into a cuisine which, although not vegetarian as such, sees no shame in serving meat free dishes. Pork is forbidden in Islam and while lamb and mutton are popular dishes, Lenten traditions ensure that vegetarian food is both imaginative and well regarded. Olives, dates, nuts, honey, yoghurt, cinnamon, coriander, fruits and cheeses are used to create nutritious meals, typically served with rice, bulgar wheat, or in North Africa, couscous. Salad is eaten at all times of the day – breakfast, lunch, dinner or inbetween – relished for its fresh flavours and cleansing the palate in the dry air,

It is a shame there don't seem to be any Iranian restaurants in London, for not only do they grow many varieties, and are true connoisseurs of rice, but their chefs are esteemed throughout the Arab world as masters of their art. In particular, Iranians are experts at stews and soups, using the dill, mint and coriander which, along with lemon, onion and garlic, are the signature flavourings of their cuisine

Turkish food by contrast is subtler, more restrained in its use of herbs and spices, letting the natural flavours of the food speak for themselves. Not surprisingly, most Middle-Eastern cooking falls between these two kitchen stools.

London has numerous Middle-Eastern restaurants, though many are of poor quality. Greek cafés are concentrated in Camden and Kentish Town, while Dalston, Stoke Newington and Newington Green are good areas to find Turkish food. The adventurous should explore the Edgware Road and Marylebone where they will be rewarded with truly amazing Lebanese and Egyptian food.

SPANISH & PORTUGUESE

I t's unlikely that a Spanish or Portuguese restaurant will have much to offer the vegetarian for like the French and the English, Iberians love to eat meat and have been lucky enough to have it in abundance. Both the Portuguese and the Spanish are fond of fish, and the former also have a taste for offal (as you will find out if you venture to SW8 where there are upwards of 20 000 Portuguese residents, mostly employed in the hotel and catering trades).

The Iberian peninsula has had a long history of invasion. Over the years Celts, Greeks, Moors and Romans have brought their influence to bear on the region. Portugal itself was a kingdom of Spain and there are still serious divisions in a country recovering from the savage rule of Franco.

Spain and Portugal were pioneers in the plunder of the New World and brought back tomatoes and potatoes, both of which have become important ingredients in their cuisines, as their rich and steamy stews prove. Portuguese cooking in particular, spicier and more exotic than the solid hearty fare of Spain, has embraced the influence of colonial Angola, Brazil and Mozambique.

These flavours arrived as a result of Iberian seafaring, and the seafaring probably explains their taste for fish. Vegetables are usually served separately from the meat, but as Iberian eaters are keen for their food to be uncomplicated and unadorned (admittedly this is more a Spanish trait), the vegetable dishes are on the whole too bland or elementary to satisfy a vegetarian.

Having said that, vegetables are eaten young and fresh in Spain and Portugal, and the fruit is of course magnificent. Despite the fact that restauranteurs from the peninsula are at the mercy of British suppliers, one should still be able to enjoy a salad or dessert. And although this won't keep the vegans happy, wonderful omelettes and tortillas (perhaps made with tender young asparagus) prove that the Spanish cook certainly has a way with an egg.

THAI

There are a ton of good Thai restaurants in London, and more seem to open every week. Some of the best Thai restaurants inthe capital are greasy spoons by day and convert to Thai at night – West London is home to plenty of these. Thai food in particular is becoming increasingly popular and influential on our eating habits. Most restaurants with an international menu will serve a Thai dish and lemon-grass, a Thai favourite, is becoming ubiquitous in good restaurants. Thai food in its turn was influenced by both Chinese and Indian cuisine, both holding strong sway throughout the region. "From the Chinese comes the balancing of five flavours – sweet, sour, hot, salty and bitter" says Jenny Linford "and from the Indian the use of spices and curry pastes".

In common with much of South East Asia the staples are rice and noodles. What seems uniquely Thai is the use of aromatics – fragrant, sweet and sour over and undertones – lemon-grass, garlic, tamarind, ginger. Lime leaves, coriander and mint. Iberian traders introduced chillies. Suffering from severe cold and depression in Australia last year (and the much lauded Aussie cuisine owes a large debt to Thai cooking) I was cured by hot and spicy Thai noodle soups. As you eat your mood lifts, your sinus clears, your mind sharpens. This is spiritual food connecting the eater with other diners and creating harmony with the world. To the Thai it is an offering, and not taken lightly. Partly because of this, Thai food looks excellent - presentation is an important part of the offering.

Thailand is predominantly Buddhist and Thais eat a lot of fish, which Buddhists throughout Asia regard as 'sea vegetables' and fit to eat. This doesn't mean that there won't be vegetable dishes on the menu – there will be – hot, tangy, exploding with the flavours of high quality fresh herbs, spices and produce. But the vegetarian should be careful: fish sauce is often used in place of soy, and dried or fermented fish (such as shrimp paste) is commonly used as a salting ingredient. If in doubt, ask, though the best Thai restaurants will indicate vegetarian dishes on the menu, and there will normally be plenty of them. Don't miss out on a food that is set (quite rightly) to become a major force on the dinner table and is well suited to the vegetarian.

RESTAURANTS

Kings Road Café

EAST LONDON

A part from the enormous quantity of half decent Indian restaurants which may afford relief, East London is notoriously poorly off for veggie restaurants. Sure, every week there is another story of a new place opening, but more often than not they're gone before you get there.

That little corner of Bethnal Green around the London Buddhist Centre is indeed an oasis, but I wonder why there is so little else. Squatney (home of 'Tap legends Nigel Tufnell and David St. Hubbins) has the greatest concentration of artists in Western Europe apparently. I can only assume these are the starving-in-a-garret type, because they don't seem to go out in the area. Perhaps the proximity of so many restaurants on Brick Lane is a disincentive to entrepreneurs. Who, after all, can compete with the one-pot-masala system ?

E1 Whitechapel

Taboon
59 Wentworth Street, Whitechapel, E1
0171 247 7079
Transport: Aldgate East LU
See Taboon on page 39 for further details.

E2 Bethnal Green

Cherry Orchard [£££]
241-245 Globe Road, Bethnal Green, E2
0181 980 6678
Transport: Bethnal Green LU
Mon/Thu/Fri 11am-4pm Tue-Wed 11am-7pm
Unlicensed
Counter/takeaway service
Non-smoking
Vegan options
Another offshoot of the London Buddhist Centre on Roman Road, the Cherry Orchard is a cheerful oasis of calm and friendliness, with its blue and yellow walls, garden out back, and inexpensive and hearty food. There are normally two main dishes to choose from (£3.75), as well as the staple baked potatoes (£2.00 with filling) and salads (£1.70-2.30). Do the local market or a meditation class and then hang out here with the papers and a lavender tea or lassi.

Thai Garden
249 Globe Road, Bethnal Green, E2
0181 981 5748
Transport: Bethnal Green LU
Lunch Mon-Fri 12-2.45 Dinner Mon-Sat 6-10.45
Licensed
Table/takeaway service
Non-smoking
Vegan options
The Thai Garden, like the national diet of its homeland, splits its menu more or less evenly between vegetable and fish dishes. It has a long standing reputation for excellence as the reviews in the window proudly advertise. The chef, Mrs. Pensri Vichit, is a maestro with mushrooms, and the Tom Khar soup (cauliflowers in coconut with galanga) is excellent. Cooking is subtle, and attention is given to enticing combinations of texture, flavour and colour. Service is formal and efficient. The fixed price menu comes in at only £7.50, and this is understandably a restaurant that people come from far and wide to visit.

RESTAURANTS

E8 Hackney

Café Alba [££]
183 Mare Street, E8
0181 985 8349
Transport: Bethnal Green LU
Mon-Fri 12-3, 6-10.30, Sat-Sun 12-10.30
Unlicensed
Table service
Smoking

Café Alba is a lot of fun. There are ever changing exhibitions on the walls, and it's a little like eating in an art gallery, though the undulating techno-trance music pumping from the kitchen, and the singing, dancing waitrons could remind you otherwise. There are always two or three vegetarian courses. The Brie and Mushroom pie was delicious, and the pastry was just the right texture. Covered in dill sauce and accompanied by buttery mashed spuds it was spot on. My partner had an over-genreous portion of Mushroom, Walnut and Broccoli stroganoff, which was a bit too creamy served with couscous that was light on couscous but heavy on raw onion, and which we left. The food here is normally interesting if rarely enlightening, but the ambience is cool, the staff matey, and I've never been disappointed.

Green Door Wholefood Café [£]
18 Ashwin Street, Dalston, E8
0171 249 6793
Transport: Dalston Junction BR
Mon-Fri 9-3
Licensed
Counter/takeaway service
Non-smoking

Situated on the ground floor of the old Reeves paint factory, this noisy vegetarian caff treats locals to inexpensive and filling dishes with an international spirit. Soups are £1.60, main courses £2.95, and salads cost between £1.20 and 2.50. The food isn't fantastic, though it is very good value for money, and the smiles from the staff are genuine enough to make any visit worthwhile.

The Thai Garden

EC

T he City proves once and for all that vegetarians cannot be reduced to dog-on-a-string stereotypes, and neither are they necessarily eccentric old ladies with heart problems. We come in all shapes and sizes, as do our wallets, and some of us even wear suits. Perhaps it's something to do with the sedentary lifestyle, but some of our desk-bound chums are eating healthily at lunch time and working out before they go home for the night.

This explains the drawback with many of the best City veg-sheds; they don't open at night and are out of the way for most of us. Amongst that strange mixture of modern buildings and ancient streets, where the origin of many place names is older than the City itself, there are two of the best restaurants in London. So take a day off, and treat yourself at The Place Below or Carnevale. Don't let the suits have all the fun!

EC1 Farringdon, Angel, Old Street

Al's Diner [££]
11-15 Exmouth Market, EC1
0171 837 4821
Transport: Angel/Farringdon LU
Mon-Fri 7-11 Sat-Sun 10-8
Licensed
Table service
Smoking
Disabled access
A roomy and recently revamped restaurant on the corner of Exmouth Market, which provides a salutary lesson on the subject of the veggie breakfast. For although Al's has a veggie breakfast (£4, and the "Super Big Veggie Breakfast" for £6) on the menu, it is basically the standard fry-up without the sausages and bacon, and therefore available in any greasy caff. I include it only as an example of seemingly veggie friendly, slightly hip cafés that in reality do us few favours. All I ask for is some bubble and squeak, and a veggie sausage or two. It doesn't take much, honest guv.

Axiom Café [£]
22 Underwood Street, EC1
0171 490 2924
Transport: Old Street LU
Mon-Fri 8.30-2.30
Unlicensed
Counter Service
Smoking
Vegan options

In the ground floor of a Victorian warehouse in a very industrial area, this is not a place to go after dark. It's just a few doors down from Friends of the Earth, with friendly staff and the walls plastered with theatre posters. Main courses cost about £3.95 (Spinach and Potato Curry on the day I went), though there are the usual jacket potatoes, salads, pizza and quiche. It seems to serve a community of locals and arty types, and could probably do with some brighter lighting to wake up the dark space.

Community Health Foundation Lunch Club [££]
188 Old Street, EC1
0171 251 4076
Transport: Old Street LU
Mon-Fri 1-2
Unlicensed
Counter service
Non-smoking
Vegan options
Those mourning the loss of East West can now find food upstairs in their old premises just down from Old Street station (and above Freshlands Wholefoods). In a renovated factory building, the Community Health Foundation runs cookery classes and also offers a three course wholefood lunch, promising 'highest quality organic ingredients'. The price is a bit steep at £8 per head, and you'll have to book in advance, but numbers are limited and the food is good if unadventurous.

RESTAURANTS

Cranks [££]
5 Cowcross Street, EC1
0171 490 4870
Transport: Farringdon LU
See Cranks on page [?] for further details

Carnevale
135 Whitecross Street, Barbican, EC1
0171 250 3452
Transport: Old Street/Barbican LU
Mon-Fri 10-10.30
Licensed
Counter & waiter/takeaway service
Vegan options
Carnevale is not easy to find, but well worth the effort. From the crisp, Conranesque design to the friendly service and excellent food, this is a standout veggie sandwich bar and restaurant. On ciabatta, baguette or granary, sandwiches are only £2.00, while salads in cute cardboard boxes are priced between £2.50 and 3.00. There are tables out back where you can enjoy a set meal (when we visited it featured a delightful Asparagus and Mascarpone Risotto) for only £8.50. It warms my heart that Carnevale exists, but breaks it that there aren't more like it. 'Carnevale' comes from the Latin, meaning 'removal of meat' from the diet during Lent. So there.

EC2 City of London

The Place Below [££]
St. Mary-Le-Bow, Cheapside, EC2
0171 329 0789
Transport: Bank LU
Mon-Fri 7.30-2.30
Unlicensed
Counter/takeaway service
Non-smoking
Vegan options
Veggie City dwellers are well served with eating places, and this is the best. St. Mary-Le-Bow was gutted by the Great Fire, restored by Wren, and destroyed again during WWII. Now it houses The Place Below, not cheap, but very busy, very noisy, and garnering unanimously good reviews. Bread is baked on the premises, and their meals are based on good fresh produce with a Mediterranean accent. The blue cheese with red onions, roast peppers, olives, sugar snap peas and croutons was mouth-watering, and their salads are highly imaginative. Things must be going well – chef Bill Sewell has just produced a book, "Food From The Place Below", and opened the St. Marylebone Café (see p.35). Ask about the Thursday night gourmet specials where Sewell really rocks out food-wise.

EC3 Aldgate, Tower of London

Futures Take-away [££]
8 Botolph Alley, EC3
0171 623 4529
Transport: Monument LU
Mon-Fri 7.30-10 11.30-3
Counter service/Vegan options/Delivery service
A tiny sandwich counter halfway along a grim alleyway in the heart of the City, normally with a snail-like queue of besuited and overworked bank clerks outside. Futures offer a small daily choice of a soup, a hot-pot, a bake, and four salads, all to be taken away as there is no seating. They also offer a free delivery service to local businesses on orders over £10.

Carnevale

NORTH LONDON

N orth London is the great Guardian-reader land – home to Nick Hornby's Arsenal, Hunter Davies' Tottenham, that great forgotten monument to communication at Alexandra Palace, and every second university lecturer in London. It's a great area for walking, or sitting in cafés and pubs, but not so hot for a night out, and there are perhaps three decent cinemas covering all 22 postal districts. Despite some wonderful Charles Holden tube stations on the Piccadilly lines, the architecture leaves much to be desired, and Pevsner's 'Buildings of England: Middlesex' (which covers much of the area) is the thinnest of the volumes in his series.

Having said all that, there is an excellent choice of places the vegetarian to eat – not only in number, but in style. Finchley is good for Indian and Chinese, Upper Street and Chapel Market have always been dominated by eating places and can boast enticing veggie alternatives to the trendy meateries, whilst the Crouch End/Finsbury Park axis offers cheap South Indian and expensive international café culture.

My favourite place to be stranded, desperate for good food, is Stoke Newington Church Street. The area is changing fast and seems to suffer from a curious schizophrenia; although the local shops are going upmarket, every second passer by is a student and the Police arrest people without body-piercings. There is a community feel that is missing in Crouch End for instance, and a fabulous jewel like Rasa is enough to engender civic pride in any neighbourhood.

N1 Islington, King's Cross

Bennett & Luck [£]
52 Islington Park Street, N1
0171 226 3422
Transport: Highbury & Islington LU/BR
Mon-Fri 9-7 Sat 9-6.30
Unlicensec
Counter/takeaway service
Non-smoking
Vegan options
A long thin wholefood store, where at the back you'll find a lunch counter and a selection of mis-matched chairs and tables. It's cheap (very) and cheerful, and £1.30 will buy you some delicious pizza to chew on while you browse the Gurjiyeff you bought from the interesting book section. They also do salads and spuds.

Candid Café [££]
3 Torrens Street, Islington, N1
0171 278 9368
Transport: Angel LU
Mon-Sat 12-10
Unlicensed BYO
Table service
Smoking
Part of the Candid Arts Trust behind the old Angel underground Station, the Candid café is up some rickety stairs on the first floor of an old warehouse. Meals are both meat and veg, but the non-meat choices are pretty good, especially the pasta. Service is shambolically good humoured, but it fits in well with the general atmosphere and the jumble of old chairs and tables. Peaceful and relaxing, try the Candid to recharge your batteries.

Candid Café

Charminar [£]

21 Chapel Market, Islington, N1
0171 278 9322
7 days 12-12
Transport: Angel LU
Licensed
Table service
Smoking
Vegan options

The second and newest of Chapel Market's Indian veggies, knocking out the South Indian favourites at bargain prices. Their eat as much as you can handle lunch time buffet, with over twenty dishes to choose from, comes in at £3.25, and the dinner deal is £3.50. "Book early" they said, but it was pretty empty when I got there.

Indian Veg Bhel-Poori House [£]

92/93 Chapel Market, N1 9EX
0171 837 4607
Transport: Angel LU
7 days 12-3 6-11pm
Licensed
Table service/Smoking/Vegan options

The Indian Veg is clean, spacious and open, and the management take great pride in their veggie and vegan fare. A favourite with local workers, as evidenced by the business-suits, the Indian Veg is also justly proud that their restaurant is the haunt of both "Miss Asia and Miss Philippines". Portions are large, and the thalis varied. Most eaters go for the extensive "as much as you can eat" buffet, which is actually cheaper now than it was when I first ate there. The menu is entertainment in itself - sections are headed "Food Power", "Food For Thought", and the International section includes the enticing "Bran Sticks Meal". Very good value.

Pasha [££]

301 Upper Street, N1
0171 226 1454
Transport: Angel LU
Mon-Thu 12-2.30 6-11.30 Fri-Sat 12-2.30 6-12 Sun 12-11
Licensed
Table service
Smoking
Vegan options
Disabled access

The deep blue exterior of the Pasha gives way to a cool and minimal dining area, with simple, well designed crockery and cutlery. Service is polite and formal, and the staff are 'professional' waiters (as opposed to 'out-of-work-actor' waiters). 50% of the menu is vegetarian with a long list of veggie hors d'oeuvres and meze (the 'mucver' — courgette and cheese fritters — are outstanding). The management are accommodating and will normally change set menus to suit, or cook for unusual dietary needs. A luxurious pleasure and a far cry from the studied informality of Neal's Yard.

RESTAURANTS

Pizza Express [£]
335 Upper Street, Angel, N1
0171 226 9542
Transport: Angel LU
See Kettners on page [?] for further details

Rye Wholefoods [£]
35a Myddleton Street, Angel N1
0171 278 5878
Transport: Angel LU
Mon-Fri 9.30-6 Sat 10.30-2.30
Unlicensed
Counter/takeaway service
Non-smoking
Vegan options
Serving the students of City University, as well as local workers, this little wholefood shop has an excellent lunch bar and a small table where you can yaffle down your pasta salad or date slice. Simple, cheerful and good.

N2 East Finchley

Mahavir Sweet Mart [£]
127c High Road, East Finchley, N2
0181 883 4595
Transport: East Finchley LU
Tues-Sat 11.00-8.30, Sun 10.30-6.30
Takeaway service
No smoking
Vegan options.
The Mahavir is a real treat, and has been based in Finchley for 23 years. Indian snacks are freshly cooked and delivered hot to your paw. The sweets sit on colourful display amongst sequined religious pictures and incense sticks. Their own brand chilli potato crisps are too hot to handle, and their samosas crisp and full of vegetables. Potato and onion chops were crunchy on the outside and soft and spicy on the inside with a delicate hint of coconut. The mixed vegetable curry wasn't quite as good, but it was huge portion for £2.00. The owners are strict Hindus and very friendly and informative about Hindu vegetarianism and Indian food.

Mandarin [£££]
152 High Road, East Finchley, N2
0181 444 0012
Transport: East Finchley LU
Mon-Sat 12-2 5-11.30
Sun 12-2 6-11.30
Licensed
Table/takeaway service
Smoking
Vegan options
Mandarin take pride in their vegetarian menu and announce it with huge hand-written posters in the windows. As is typical of Chinese vegetarian food, much of it imitates meat – vegetarian shark fin soup for instance. Also available are stuffed oyster mushrooms with cheese and coriander, and a generous selection of veggie hors d'oeuvres. The veggie set menu changes every month. The Mandarin is generally very quiet, so do call first – restaurants (especially underused ones) come and go in this part of London.

Mahavir Sweet Mart

N3 Finchley Central

Rani [£££]
7 Long Lane, Finchley, N3 2PR
0181 349 4386
Transport: Finchley Central LU
Opening hours vary (please check)
Licensed
Table/takeaway service
Smoking
Vegan options
The food at Rani has always been satisfactory, though it isn't especially good value for money. We had two Cobra beers (always excellent), bhel poori mixed with garlic and tamarind, which was delicious, and mixed bhajis (a very small plate), with tasty coriander chutney. Stuffed aubergine with potato was rather spicy, and needed a raita (which tasted like shop bought yoghourt) to cool it down. The Banana Mehti lacked fenugreek and the Nan was disappointingly meagre. The menu however was well laid out, and you'll know exactly what you're eating, even if you're blind (there is also a Braille menu). Service can be a bit clinical, and the waiters were not good at explaining the dishes (YTS trainees, we wondered ?). The cutlery and crockery was awful, pseudo-Woolworths with naff patterns, which you can forgive in a cheaper restaurant with less of a reputation, but we felt like we were eating in a pizza restaurant – especially with the red metal chairs, and glass table tops. The owner made things worse by boasting that Rani was "in all the restaurant guides". A huge disappointment, and one senses a restaurant resting on it's laurels.
also at:
3 Hill Street, Richmond TW9
0181 322 2322

N4 Finsbury Park

Jai Krishna [£]
161 Stroud Green Road, N4
0171 272 1680
Transport: Finsbury Park LU
Mon-Sat 12-2 5.30-11pm
Unlicensed/BYO
Table service
Smoking
Vegan options
This noisy canteen type restaurant is somewhere I often came as a student. It has a good natured clientele, is very cheap and was always reliable for interesting and tasty South Indian food. My last visit wasn't quite so good. The owners were rattled by a hectic St. Valentine's Day crowd, and we weren't allowed to order one pariticular dish as it was "too busy". There was no heating, and the atmosphere was far too smokey. The tip tray annoyed me, there is no service and meals are ordered at the counter. No doubt we came on a bad night – the lemon rice was still as delicious and subtle as ever.

N6 Highgate

Café Vert [£]
269a Archway Road, Highgate N6
0181 348 7666
Transport: Highgate LU
Tue-Fri 10-9 Mon & Sat 10-3.30 Sun 12-3.30
Licensed
Counter service
Smoking
Vegan options
Jacksons Lane is a community theatre and arts space with a strong programme of innovative and challenging work. Within it, chef Marc Joseph is building a reputation for himself as an imaginative and consistent vegetarian cook. However I wonder whether Jacksons Lane can keep him. It doesn't deserve to. Maybe I just visited on a bad day, for the eating area, part of a larger open plan hall/waiting area, was swimming in the ill-mannered and spoiled offspring of middle-class North London. My pasta bake (£3.50)

tasted wonderful, as did a luscious thick banana milkshake (£1), but I could hardly get the food to my mouth without a pre-teen hooligan in 'Gap for Kids' launching himself across my table, his Birkenstocked mother screeching "Julian! Come and play nicely with Edwina". I felt like I was trapped in a Posy Simmons' cartoon.

N8 Hornsey

Planet Y [£]
Hornsey YMCA, 184 Tottenham Lane, Crouch End, N8
0181 340 6088
Transport: Turnpike Lane LU/Hornsey BR
Mon-Fri 12-7.30 Sat 11-4
Unlicensed
Counter service
Non-smoking
Vegan options

This little known vegodrome is tucked away in the Fitness Centre recreation area of the YMCA in Hornsey. Though they must do a roaring trade in water and isotonic Lucozade, there is also solid sustenance in the form of filled pittas, salads and a main course special, which on the day I visited was bulgar chilli with rice.

World Café [££]
130 Crouch Hill, N8 9DY
0181 340 5635
Transport: Crouch Hill BR
7 Days 9.30-11
Licensed
Table service
Smoking
Vegan options
Disabled access

Despite its name, the World Café had a distinctly Mediterranean feel the afternoon we visited. It does do meat dishes but also has a fair selection of non-meat choices, though these often include cheese. Service is friendly, though not overbearing, and the mood is unhurried, which is fine if you're already seated but makes getting a table hard work at busy times. The desserts are excellent, beautifully served and, almost uniquely, the World Café serves some lively non alcoholic cold drinks like citron pressé (fresh lemon juice with sugar). A favourite haunt of Eurhythmics' Dave Stewart who has a studio across the road, but I wouldn't let that put you off.

Oshobasho Café

RESTAURANTS

N10 Muswell Hill

Oshobasho Café[££]

Highgate Wood, Muswell Hill Road, N10 3JN
0181 444 1505
Transport: Highgate LU
Tue-Fri 9.00 - 1 hour before sunset
Sat-Sun 8.30-1 hour before sunset
open Bank Holidays
Licensed
Counter service
Non-smoking
Vegan Options

Set in an old cricket pavilion in the middle
of Highgate Wood, Oshobasho is a little
oasis of calm in the bustle of London,
especially if the weather is good and you sit
in the garden. Highgate villagers sit around
munching croissants and reading broadsheet
newspapers. The choice is of soups, salads
and filled breads, their cakes are pretty
good too, but the real deal is not the food –
it's the restful atmosphere. The coffee is
excellent although not cheap at £1.20.

N16 Stoke Newington

Magpie and Stump [£££]

132 Stoke Newington Church Street, N16
0171 254 0959
Mon-Sat 12-3.30 7-10.30 Sun 12-3
Transport: Stoke Newington BR
Licensed
Counter service
Smoking

This is a great part of London for non-
omnivores, and though this large corner
pub doesn't look too promising, it actually
offers good veggie scran as either pub grub,
or in the Scallywag restaurant upstairs. The
ambience here is relaxed, wood-panelled
and easy, and there is a garden for the
summer. There is meat on the menu, but
the vegetarian dishes are nothing to be
ashamed of if slightly expensive. Get
yourself a whopping great pint of London
Pride and use it to wash down food which is
modern British with more than a hint of
Mediterranean .

Rasa [£££]

55 Stoke Newington Church Street, Stoke
Newington, N16
0171 249 0344
Transport: Stoke Newington BR
7 days 12-2.30 6-midnight
Licensed
Table/takeaway service
Non-smoking
Vegan options

Rasa was wonderful, and we weren't the
only people to think so. Despite booking,
we had to wait 30 minutes for a table, but
were kept happy by manager Alison who
brought us papadums and chatted. The food
is from Kerala, a tropical region of south-
western India where a tradition of trading
has left the cuisine with Arab, Chinese and
European influences. Portions are just the
right size for the subtle flavours. Mysore
Bonda (potatoes, herbs and spices in chick
pea batter) was tangy, and a dish of
mangoes and bananas cooked in yoghurt
(Moru Kachiathu) was a treat for the
tongue. Although the lassi was
disappointingly lukewarm on a hot day, it
was refreshing to sit in such a welcoming
atmosphere and watch the road ragers
simmer in a congested Church Street
outside.

NW1 Camden Town, Euston, Marylebone

While Camden and Euston are
probably your best bet for a cut-
price post-gig curry, if you go a little further
– up past Marine Ices to Chalk Farm – you
can find some of the best Chinese food in
London. Hampstead is terribly
disappointing, as is Primrose Hill, but go
further out to those fearful regions north of
Baker Street on the Bakerloo line and you
are in for a treat.

Kilburn and Willesden may not seem to
have much to offer except friendly (and not
so friendly) Irish pubs, and the occasionally
exhilarating tube ride home amidst tanked

up England football fans, or worse (I was once trapped on a tube train at Kilburn with three hundred Bros-ettes!). But there you'll find two excellent Indian restaurants, popular with locals – always a good sign – and friendly as well.

You shouldn't rule out a trip to the Yaohan Japanese shopping Plaza either, though you'll need a car. Even if you choose not to eat the amazing Japanese pizzas at Obeno, you'll discover a fascinating slice of London life you'd never have thought existed.

Chutneys [££]

124 Drummond Street, Euston, NW1
0171 388 0604
Transport: Euston/Euston Square LU
Licensed
Table service
Smoking
Vegan options

Chutneys is one of three Indian veggie restaurants on Drummond Street (see also Diwana and Ravi Shankar). There are four sections to the menu, each offering food from a different region of India - Bombay, Gujurat, Madras and Western India. It is big (120 seats) and cheap (lunchtime buffet is £4.95, and evening set meals are only £8.95), but not particularly memorable.

Diwana [££]

121-123 Drummond Street, Euston, NW1
0171 387 5556
Euston/Euston Square LU
Unlicensed
Table service
Smoking
Vegan options

"Traditional tasty snacks from Chowpatty Beach of Bombay" reads the motto outside, and Diwana does indeed rely on a minimal menu of Indian veggie treats – bhel poori, dosas and thalis. Very cheap (the daily special is £4.50 and lunchtime buffet only £3.95), but with a reputation for slow and inept service.

Ravi Shankar [££]

133-135 Drummond Street, Euston, NW1
0171 388 6458
Transport: Euston/Euston Square LU
Licensed
Table service
Smoking
Vegan options

Ravi Shankar has the most interesting décor on Drummond Street, with its sandy brown earth tones and bare wooden furniture, it looks more Mediterranean than your average curry house. Open 365 days a year, it seems pretty busy for most of them and is most people's favourite Drummond Street haunt. The menu is again divided into four regional sections and there is always plenty of choice for vegans. Very cheap, and it really isn't worth going elsewhere unless you have to.

St. Marylebone Café [££]

17 Marylebone Road, NW1
0171 935 6374
Transport: Baker St./Regents Park LU
Mon-Fri 8.30-3
Unlicensed
Counter service
Non-smoking
Vegan options

Deep in the crypt of the eponymous church, the St. Marylebone Café is as light, clean and crisp as you'd expect from a Bill Sewell project (he also operates the wonderful Place Below in the City, see page 26). Everything gives off a flavour of health, seating is fastidiously arranged, and there are dinky hand-painted hangings on the walls. On offer are a small selection of salads, baked spuds and quiches, and although the food was slightly uninspired by Sewell's own high standards, it wasn't stodgy or bland. A huge plus point was the absence of background music (how I've grown to hate the sound of supper club jazz), and I found the café atmosphere soothing and meditative.

RESTAURANTS

Ravi Shankar

Camden Market, NW1

Transport: Camden Town/Chalk Farm LU

As Andrew Kershman points out in The London Market Guide "The markets in Camden Town – and there are at least six – have established a reputation as a sort of Mecca for those in search of street cred". In fact, for tourists between the ages of 16 and 25, Camden is the top London attraction, it's nearest rival being Madame Tussauds! This means that the place is awash with adolescent wannabes looking for that great British export – yoof culture.

Serious shoppers and locals go there on a Friday when the Japanese girls and the hair plaiters are visiting the London Dungeon, and it's as good a place as any for veggie fast foods. The Camden Lock and Stables Market areas (Saturday and Sunday only) are the best for food – Japanese, Indian, Caribbean, Chinese and Thai – often from the same vendor. The Stables food stalls often have seating and prices, despite the tourists, are normally pretty good. Food quality varies, but there are usually one or two gems if you don't settle for the first thing you see.

NW3 Hampstead

Manna [££]

4 Erskine Road, Primrose Hill, NW3
0171 722 8028
Transport: Chalk Farm LU
7 days 6.30-11
Licensed
Table service
Non-smoking
Vegan options

Behind an old glass porch is Manna, started as a community restaurant in 1968 (they'd have you believe they're the oldest vegetarian in London), and still plodding along. It has a veggie-rustic look, and the same earthy-worthy feel as Cranks, but the food here is more interesting. Mediterranean, Latin-American and Oriental flavours influence the menu, as they do at many of the better veggie eateries. I guess the geographical position makes a difference to the price, because Manna is not cheap and neither is it particularly good value for money. Perhaps they should move to Camden? The sweets are good though.

Vegetarian Cottage [£££]

91 Haverstock Hill, Chalk Farm, NW3
0171 586 1257
Transport: Belsize Park/Chalk Farm LU
Mon-Sat 6-11.30 Sun 12-3.30 6-11.30
Licensed
Table/takeaway service
Smoking
Vegan options

Vegetarian Cottage is widely acknowledged as not only the best Chinese vegetarian restaurant in London, but one of the best Chinese full stop. Although it sells one or two seafood dishes, it specialises in Chinese vegetarian food in the Buddhist tradition. There is nothing simple or mundane about the fare on offer here. Their 'imitation fish' or 'vegetarian duckling' are not dishes you'll make at home, but are skillful counterfeits made from lentils or soya beans. Their ingredients are unusual and for the adventurous, as exciting as a voyage into the heart of China itself - black moss and oyster mushrooms for instance. Perhaps the most surprising thing is that Vegetarian Cottage is far from expensive. The Sunday 'all you can eat buffet' is only £8.00.

NW6 Kilburn/West Hampstead

Geeta [££]
57-59 Willesden Lane, Willesden NW6
0171 624 1713
Transport: Kilburn LU/Brondesbury Park BR
Mon-Sat 11.30-3 5.30-11.45
Licensed
Table/takeaway service
Smoking
Willesden never seems very alluring, but if you must make a trip, do so for the splendid vegetarian food of Kerala and Tamil Nadu, which Geeta really make a meal of. The restaurant seems popular both with the public and the press if the reviews and full tables are anything to go by, and even if the surroundings are somewhat grim, the staff are not. Although there are meat dishes on the menu, you should not let that put you off – take some meat-eating friends, though if they too don't plump for the green banana curry, they'll be very foolish.

Surya [££]
59-61 Fortune Green Road, West Hampstead, NW6
Transport: West Hampstead LU/BR
7 days 12-2.30 6-10.30
Licensed
Table/takeaway service
Smoking
Vegan options
A very small restaurant, run by the Gujurati Tiwari family, and which is always packed. The menu however changes daily, so there is never a shortage of new dishes to excite the tastebuds. Mrs. Tiwari, the chef, offers nice little touches that other restaurants at this budget level forget - the sprinkled fresh coriander for instance. Exactly the sort of neighbourhood veggie restaurant one should be going out of one's way to support – but the regulars don't need me to tell them.

NW7 Mill Hill

Good Earth [££££]
143 The Broadway, Mill Hill, NW7
0181 959 7011
Transport: Mill Hill Broadway BR
See Good Earth Knightsbridge [see page 45] for further details.

Abeno [££]
Yaohan Plaza, 399 Edgware Road, Kingsbury, NW9
0181 205 1131
Transport: Colindale LU
Mon-Fri 12-2.45 6-10 Sat-Sun 12-10
Licensed
Table/takeaway service
Non-smoking
Yaohan Plaza is one of my favourite places in London - a vast Japanese hypermarket mall with a Sega games hall, Japanese bookshops (where my friend Simon picks up his monster-books), and a super Nipponese food hall. It also houses one excellent restaurant, Abeno, the only restaurant in Europe to serve Okonomi-yaki, a kind of omelette/pizza which is cooked on a hot plate set into your table. The base of the omelette is cabbage, egg and a dough made from yam and flour. This is piled high with vegetables, seaweeds, noodles, etc. and then topped with mayonnaise and special sauce in beautiful concentric circles. It is very popular with Japanese businessmen (in Japan it's a cheap fast food). It's not too expensive here either, and the restaurant is an ideal location for an office party or family get-together.

Abeno

NW11 Golders Green
Taboon Bakery [£]
17 Russell Parade, Golders Green Road, Golders Green, NW11
0181 455 7451
Transport: Brent Cross LU
Sun-Fri 10-Midnight
Counter/takeaway service
Non-smoking
Vegan options
An open plan Kosher bakery with a small counter from which you can purchase a variety of breads, sambusa and falafel. Their falafel filled pittas with salad are a favourite with local teenagers and a bargain at only £2.00.

Pizza Express [££]
94 Golders Green Road, Golders Green, NW11
0181 455 9556
Transport: Golders Green LU
See Kettners on page 53 for further details.

Pizza Express [££]
194 Haverstock Hill, Belsize Park, NW3
0171 794 6777
Transport: Belsize Park LU
See Kettners on page 53 for further details.

Pizza Express [££]
227 Finchley Road, West Hampstead, NW3
0171 794 5100
Transport: West Hampstead LU/BR
See Kettners on page 53 for further details.

Sabras [££]
263 High Road, Willesden, NW10
0181 459 0340
Transport: Dollis Hill LU
Tue-Sun 12.30-10.30
Licensed
Table/takeaway service
Smoking
Vegan options
The Desais, from the Gujurati coastal town of Surat, have been in Willesden since the early seventies, and their popular bright and airy café serves up the dosas, thalis and bhel poori at excellent prices for such an attractive and inviting establishment. The owner's obvious pride in their restaurant comes across in the quality of both the food and the welcome. There have been rumours of closure, but hopefully the Desais will survive and Sabras continue to supply Willesden with delectable vegetarian Indian food.

SOUTH LONDON

I t's no wonder that people are wary of travelling south of the river. There are only 21 tube stations, the suburban railways are unreliable and stop too early, and the driving is comparable to that of Buenos Aires or Rome.

Still, we Southerners like to keep it that way. For us Peckham is a pleasure, and there's nowhere as bright as Brixton. And hey, we may not have many places to eat, but they're all pretty good. It was the welcome and the fine cuisine at Heather's that kept me going through the long hard slog of researching Vegetarian London, and that impressed itself on my mind as the pinnacle of achievement for a small neighbourhood café. And we can be justly proud of Mantanah - hidden from Northerners under a railway bridge, and promising little from outside, this most civilised of Thai restaurants is a foodie paradise.

SE1 Walworth, Southwark

Imperial Tandoori [£££]
48 Kennington Road, SE1
0171 928 4153
Transport: Lambeth North LU
7 days 12-2.30 6-12
Licensed
Table/takeaway service
Smoking
The Imperial is a favourite with Parliamentary members of all persuasions, with framed letters on the walls as evidence. Don't let that put you off. This quiet, rather elegant South London feeding hole, takes its name from the nearby War Museum (which commemorates, amongst its other exhibits, the 70, 000 Indians and Pakistanis who gave their lives in the two World Wars), and is a good place to stop off on the way home. Although the menu is fairly meaty, there is a good choice of veggie main and side dishes. The staff are young, friendly and happy to talk about their food.

Ivory Arch Tandoori [£]
80-82 Walworth Road, Elephant & Castle SE1
0171 703 0182
Transport: Elephant & Castle LU/BR
Mon-Thurs 12-2.30, 6-12.30; Fri 12-2, 6-2;
Sat 6-2; Sun6-12.30
Ivory Arch operate a delivery service for Vegetarian Indian food. See entry under Other Services (page 82)

Jumbleys [£]
Butler's Wharf Business Centre, Curlew Street, Butler's Wharf, SE1
0171 403 8911
Transport: London Bridge LU/BR
Mon-Fri 7-4 Sat-Sun 9-1
Table/takeaway service
Smoking
Surrounded by the glories of the Conran 'Gastrodrome', Jumbleys may appear rather humble and declassé. Set back from the Thames in the old industrial reaches of Butler's Wharf, it's unyuppified and certainly not somewhere the serious foodie will head for but, boy, does Jumbleys serve a good veggie breakfast. Sitting amongst the framed posters of Millwall you'll be presented with a huge plate of bubble and squeak, veggie sausage, beans, mushrooms, eggs and tomatoes, all topped off with tea and toast (£3.20). Never overcooked, and dished up with smiles and newspapers, Jumbleys rarely disappoints. Chris Evans, who lives at nearby Cinnamon Wharf, is a regular.

Pizza Express [££]
Chapter House, Montague Close, SE1
0171 378 6446
Transport: London Bridge LU/BR
See Kettners on page 53 for further details

SE5 Camberwell

Carrot Café [££]

53 Denmark Hill, Camberwell, SE5
0171 277 2120
Transport: Denmark Hill BR
Tue-Thu 9-6 Fri-Sat 9-5 Sun 9-5 7-12
Unlicensed/BYO
Table/takeaway service
Smoking
Vegan options

A workers' co-operative that grew out of Brixton's Cooltan, the (Camberwell) Carrot has been open since Spring '96, and was two years in the planning, the co-op doing their own self-build conversion. The produce is 80-90% organic, and the menu is veggie-international. "We tried to open the sort of café we wanted to go to", I was told, "so our food tries to bring out the flavours and aroma of our produce". Lunch costs around £4.00 and dinner £6.50. The workers obviously bring the optimistic DIY Cooltan ideology with them and so I wish them luck.

SE8 Deptford

Heathers Café-Bistro [££]

190 Trundleys Road, Deptford, SE8
0181 691 6665
Transport: South Bermondsey BR/New Cross Gate LU/Surrey Quays LU
Wed-Sat from 7.00 Sun 12.30-4.00
Unlicensed/BYO
Counter service
Non-smoking
Vegan options
Disabled access

Whenever during the course of writing this book, I despaired over yet another burnt and glutinous 'bake', I thought lovingly of Heathers, a sweet idyll of "what-things-should-be-like", tucked away in a South London back street. The idea is simple. An 'all you can eat' three course buffet for only £7.95. But because Heather's is modest and miniature, the food is made up in small quantities and doesn't have time to atrophy or lose its freshness. Although the spinach and rice soup was fairly ordinary, the homemade lemonade was tartly refreshing and we wolfed down portions of Cuban fruit curry and spicy chick peas. Service was friendly and helpful, and everyone seemed to be enjoying themselves. Heather's often organise themed evenings as fund-raisers for various causes, or barbecues and women only nights. Their newsletter is an island of sanity too, with lots of news, jokes at their own expense and sound advice. And hey ... arrive on a bike and they give you a free cold drink. Thank heaven for Heather's.

SE10 Greenwich

Escaped [££]

141 Greenwich South Street, Greenwich SE10
0181 692 5826
Transport: Lewisham/Greenwich BR
Mon-Sat 10-10.30 Sun 12-10.30
Unlicensed/BYO
Counter service
Smoking

Escaped is perfect if you want to read the newspaper or play chess while you eat - one of the old school of vegetarian restaurants built for an imagined community that sometimes materialised and sometimes didn't. Escaped seems to have one, who come largely for their splendid desserts, though main courses are of reasonable quality (veggie-international style) and none of it will put you out of pocket (three courses should cost around £10). Children run around, there are posters and postcards on sale, and the music isn't too intrusive. More of a social than a culinary experience.

SE11 Kennington

Oval Café [£]

52-54 Kennington Oval, London SE11
0171 582 0080
Transport: Oval LU
Lunch Mon-Fri 12-2.30pm Dinner Thu-Sat
5.30-11 Sun 5.30-10.30
Licensed
Counter service
Smoking

Pre-theatre or cricket, the Oval Café is a possible stop off for veggie specials, big salads, and homemade soups. The food is not especially interesting and the staff were rather surly and confused when we visited. However the atmosphere is usually friendly and relaxed, there is always something interesting to look at on the walls and it is very, very cheap. Try the spicy West Indian stews which are chunky and flavoursome.

SE25 Norwood

Mantanah [£££]

2 Orton Buildings, Portland Road, South
Norwood, SE25
0181 771 1148
Transport: Norwood Junction BR
Tue Sat 6.30-11 Sun 6.30-10.30
Licensed
Table/takeaway service
Smoking
Vegan options

We felt rather down at heel arriving at the Mantanah, a wonderful Thai restaurant run by husband and wife team Tym and Tony Yeoh. However, despite being dressed in jeans and t-shirts we were offered hot towels and treated with courtesy. Being Buddhist, Thai's eat a lot of vegetarian dishes, and the menu here reflects that. We had Pad Tai Je (noodles) with Somtom, a hot papaya salad which chased out our spring snuffles. The dishes have some strange names – 'Golden Bag' turned out to be a parcel of barley and rice, wrapped and deep fried like a small samosa – but you should be adventurous. You won't be disappointed. Washed down with Thai beer (Singha) this was a deliciously hot and sumptuous dining experience, and not over expensive. Check out the VW Beetle toilet roll dispensers too!

SOUTH WEST LONDON

Almost as varied in climate and diet as the Indian sub-continent, South west London stretches from Westminster and Knightsbridge to Barnes, Tooting and Wimbledon. Not surprisingly then, this is the area to find the widest possible choice of vegetarian food. While Paul Gayler at the Lanesborough serves a fascinating international menu in sumptuous surroundings, he'd be the first to agree that a trip to Tooting and the Kastoori is also worthwhile. An evening at the ICA offers a cheap central London night out with good food, and you'll get great lunches in a variety of establishments in Brixton – from Ethiopian to Mediterranean. South-west London has much to offer the veg-head from the relaxing hassle-free atmosphere of Wholemeal or Tumbleweeds, to the cluster of inexpensive East African Asian establishments around the High Street in Tooting.

SW1 Westminster, Pimlico, Victoria

Institute of Contemporary Arts [££]
The Mall, London, SW1Y
0171 930 8535
Transport: Piccadilly Circus/Charing Cross LU
7 days 12-3 5.30-11
Licensed
Counter service
Smoking
For such a hotbed of confrontational creativity and innovation, the ICA café is surprisingly cheap and unpretentious. The Institute is located in a vast Nash terrace near Buck House, and its café housed in an arched cellar, hung with photos of the great artists (from Picasso to Basquiat) whose work has been shown there. The café specialises in both vegetarian and Italian food, and it is invariably very good. Always on the menu are soups (£1.20), Nut Loaf, and Deep Pan Quiche (£2.00 each). Veggie main courses are £4.95, normally either pasta or polenta based, and the salads are good value for money – huge plates of taste, texture and colour for only £3.00. Afterwards the energised can play on the bar football table (tantalisingly placed just outside the café), while the more adventurous take in a Japanese film in the Cinemathèque.

The Lanesborough [££££]
1 Lanesborough Place, Hyde Park Corner, SW1X
0171 259 5599
Transport: Hyde Park Corner LU
7 days 12-12
Licensed
Table service
Smoking
Vegan options
Chef Paul Gayler is something of a maverick, single-handedly dragging vegetarian eating into the 1990's. He has been creating haute veggie cuisine for over ten years and, having worked in Singapore, in an Indian restaurant and at the Hilton, Gayler knows exactly what he's doing. Eating at The Lanesborough is a total experience. The restaurant is in a glass roofed conservatory, modelled on the Brighton Pavilion and sumptuously decorated with Chinoiserie and sofas. Don't be overawed by the surroundings: the Lanesborough is a lot of fun. While a jazz trio tinkles through the standards, couples take to the floor for a tango, and the young and friendly waiting staff whiz around efficiently.
The food is something else - when Gayler created his first seven course vegetarian menu, the media were baffled, and he recognises now that "it was quite revolutionary for its time". Gayler is at the top of his profession, but hasn't rested on his laurels, and unlike most traditional (and

many vegetarian chefs) sees working with vegetables as a way of extending his repertoire and challenging his skills. Flavours come not only from the veggie friendly cuisines of the Middle and Far East (Tabouleh and smooth, oily houmous, or delicate noodles with perfectly stir fried peppers), or from Italy, but also from France (our wild mushroom and coriander soup was mind-meltingly aromatic). My favourites, and a jewel in Gayler's crown, are the sorbets. These can only be eaten with closed eyes, and I felt I'd died and gone to Heaven.

Pizza on the Park [£££]
11 Knightsbridge, SW1
0171 235 5550
Transport: Hyde Park Corner LU
See Kettners on page 53 for further details.

Wilkins [£]
61 Marsham Street, Westminster, SW1
0171 222 4038
Transport: St. James's Park LU
Mon-Fri 8-5.30
Unlicensed
Counter/takeaway service
Non-smoking
Vegan options
Wilkins hangs off a street corner looking for all the world like an old cake shop. It does a lot of business at lunch time with local office workers and the staff of Horseferry Magistrates Court, so I go at breakfast time when it's quieter. Friendly, with higgledy-piggledy furniture which served the best years of its life in Grammar schools. Wilkins has been around for ten years or more and, although the veggie basics are little changed, it is cheap, reliable and welcoming.

Woodlands [££]
37 Panton Street, SW1
0171 839 7258
Transport: Piccadilly Circus LU
See Woodlands Wembley on page 67 for further details.

Wren at St. James's [£]
35 Jermyn Street, Piccadilly, SW1
0171 437 9419
Transport: Piccadilly Circus LU
Mon-Sat 8-7 Sun 9-5
Unlicensed
Counter service
Non-smoking
Vegan options
Set to one side of Christopher Wren's St. James's Church, this café has always had a fairly decent reputation. Bustling with tourists and with a courtyard for balmy summer days, the Wren is certainly popular. But on my visit I was greatly disappointed. The pakora were the size of cricket balls, and had the same flavour and texture, although the salads were made with fresh and interesting ingredients. The food was inexpensive but the staff were among the rudest and most disinterested I have ever come across, particularly with foreigners who were struggling with the menu. I suspect bad management somewhere along the line and, from my visit, couldn't see why anyone should rave about the place.

SW2 BRIXTON/TULSE HILL

Bah Humbug [££]
The Crypt, St. Matthew's Peace Garden, Brixton Hill, SW2
0171 738 3184
Transport: Brixton BR/LU
Mon-Fri 6-12 Sat-Sun from 11
Licensed
Table service
Smoking
Deep in the crypt of St. Matthew's Church, Bah Humbug does its best to play up the Gothic associations in this strangest of eating environments. Chairs are hewn roughly from wood, curtains are heavy dark velvets and there is one long enormous table just ripe for a mediaeval feast. The menu concentrates on fish and vegetarian dishes, and there was no meat on the menu on the day I visited.

Peter Peppers Mediterranean Café
[££]
60 Morrish Road, SW2
0181 671 5655
Transport: Streatham Hill BR
Mon-Sat 11-11
Licensing details
Table/takeaway service
Smoking
Disabled access

Peter Peppers specialise in Mediterranean and vegetarian food, and do a varied veggie breakfast, though as they don't open until 11am, I imagine they lose a bit of custom. They've come up with some imaginative mix and match combinations – veggie sausages, charcoal burgers and veggie bacon (!!). Unusual and satisfying snacks include their Mediterranean vegetables in olive oil on toast. The ubiquitous orange sponged walls contain a pleasant if somewhat noisy hidey hole, and there are plenty of other interesting vegetarian dishes on the main menu.

SW3 Chelsea, Knightsbridge

Good Earth [££££]
233 Brompton Road, Knightsbridge, SW3
0171 584 3658
Transport: South Kensington LU
Licensed
Table service
Smoking
Vegan options

The Good Earth is relatively expensive, but it is well worth a visit. Not only is the food excellent, it also has the wackiest wallpaper I've seen in a London restaurant and any of its cocktail bar rivals this side of Las Vegas. There is an extensive vegetarian menu, either imitation meat and fish dishes, such as the Faked Yellow Fish in Hot Piquant Sauce made with lentils, or the amazingly tasty vegetable dishes. The Spiced Aubergine wrapped in Seaweed was moreish, as was the Monk's Casserole but, be warned, portions are large. Good Earth also do a few Thai dishes, and their tea is the best of any Chinese restaurant in London and constantly refilled. No music either, which is a rare treat.

Kings Road Café

45

Kings Road Café [£££]
208 Kings Road, Chelsea, SW3
0171 351 1211
Transport: Sloane Square LU
Mon-Fri 10-6 Sat 12-4 Sun 1-4
Licensed
Table service
Smoking
On my visit to the first floor of Habitat, sunlight was slanting resplendently through the large rectangular windows of this former cinema. The setting is, of course, très tasteful – huge modern paintings on large white walls, excellent, well thought out furniture, olive oil on each table. Although there is normally one meat or fish dish on the restrained menu, most dishes are vegetarian with a definite Italian tang. The Café does breakfasts on weekdays, but if you can get a window seat it's just as much fun to watch the fashion victims in the Kings Road. Enjoy delicious coffee and cake while they stumble past in their Vivienne Westwood platforms.

Sydney Street Café [££]
Chelsea Farmers' Market, King's Road, SW3
0171 352 5600
Transport: South Kensington LU
7 days 9.30-5.30 (later in summer)
Licensed
Table/takeaway service
Smoking
Not always open on time, so it isn't a reliable stop off for breakfast, and if Habitat is open, you should head for the King's Road café instead. Sydney Street does have its fans however, and its summertime barbies do give veg-heads the choice of salads, vegeburgers and bangers, all for under a tenner. Be warned, it gets very busy with local shop and office workers.

SW4 Clapham

Eco [££]
162 Clapham High Street, Clapham, SW4
0171 978 1108
Transport: Clapham Common LU/Clapham High Street BR
Mon-Tue 11.30-3.30 6.30-11 Wed 6.30-11 Thu-Fri 11.30-3-30 6.30-11 Sat-Sun 11.30-4.30 6.30-11
Licensed
Table service
Smoking
This restaurant is always packed and, with a big window on Clapham High Street, is obviously a place to be seen. The opening hours seem to depend on which guide you pick up, or who you speak to on the phone, so do check first. Sandy plywood furnishings, curly copper lighting, and a media-minimalist floorboardy feeling that means 'this place is special'. Eco is not expensive, and there are always three or four non-meat pizzas, but the place is loud – music, other diners, the kitchen. Not at all relaxing, and the mobile phones make matters worse.

SW5

Balans West [£££]
239 Old Brompton Road, Earls Court, SW5
0171 244 8838
Transport: Earls Court LU
7 Days 8-1
Licensed
Table service
Smoking
A new, and altogether more user friendly branch of the Soho favourite. Kitted out in galvanised steel and varnished wood, with (comfortable) modern furniture, the menu is the same as that of the Soho Balans. There are smiles from the staff however, plenty of room and a more relaxed atmosphere. Get yourself a newspaper, sit in and chill out.

RESTAURANTS

SW6 Fulham, Parson's Green

Gardners 511 [£££]
511 Fulham Road
London SW6 1HH
0171 381 1411
Transport: Fulham Broadway LU
Tue-Sat 5-11
Licensed
Table Service
No Smoking
Vegan

Gardners is a new restaurant, only two weeks old when we visited, and the reviews are excellent. The decor is simple, perhaps slightly bleak, but the menu is fascinating. Not only are there, unusually, some very English dishes, but the menu is totally vegan. We had an excellent soup to begin with, crusty traditional pies for a tasty, solid and warming main course, and deserts which were light and fruity. Gardners have Gambrinus on tap too, a Czech beer which is timelessly Middle-European, and what's more, vegan. Let's hope this venture goes from strength to strength.

Mamta [£££]
692 Fulham Road, SW6
0171 736 5914
Transport: Parson's Green LU
Mon-Tue 6-10.30 Wed-Sat 12.30-3 6-10.30
Sun 12.30-3
Licensed
Table/takeaway service
Smoking
Vegan options

A Gujurati Jain restaurant, modern, tastefully under-designed and with an excellent reputation for vegetarian food. It's so popular I'd advise booking – once or twice I've turned up on the off chance and not been able to get a table. Staff are generally friendly and helpful, the sort who guide you through the menu, or get the chef to spice up the dish for you. Hopefully they'll direct you to their Masala Dosa – among the best in London.

Windmill Wholefoods [££]
486 Fulham Road, Fulham, SW6 5NH
0171 385 1570
Transport: Fulham Broadway LU
7 Days 10-30-10.30
Licensed
Table/takeaway service
Non-smoking
Vegan options
Disabled access

Chockablock with colour – yellow walls, worn floorboards and stacked with old biscuit tins and enamel signs – the windmill immediately puts you at your ease. The staff are friendly, and the atmosphere informal and slow. As is the service I might add, but you'll probably be in forgiving mood by this stage. Food isn't too adventurous, and we'd have liked fresh rather than dried herbs, which led to the food being bland, despite the large portions.

SW8 Vauxhall

Tea Room Des Artistes [£££]
697 Wandsworth Road, Clapham, SW8
0171 652 6526
Transport: Wandsworth Road BR
Mon-Fri 6-midnight Sat 5-midnight Sun 7-11.30
Licensed
Table service
Smoking
Vegan options

A bit too over-designed, some would say at the expense of the food, though I've a suspicion that many dislike the Tea Room clientele (generally loud, obnoxious and yuppie) more than the place itself. The décor is crisp and modern with retro touches. There is champagne for sale to wash down a reasonably sized menu of internationally influenced food. Main courses cost around £6, but are normally uninspired variants of stew, stroganoff or curry – the quickly cooked, fresh and the lively has evidently been overlooked in favour of the slowly cooked and frankly mushy.

SW9 Stockwell/Brixton

Asmara [££]
386 Coldharbour Lane, Brixton, SW9
0171 737 4144
Transport: Brixton LU/BR
Mon-Sat 11-11.30 Sun 6-12
Licensed
Table service
Smoking
Vegan options

Asmara is an unassuming and friendly restaurant, used as a pop-in centre for local Ethiopians and Eritreans, whose food it serves at cheap prices and with big smiles. Strange music tinkled from the speakers, organs and pianos, and the décor is shambolically welcoming. Not knowing our 'shiro' from our 'temtemo', we asked for advice. There are 6 or 7 veggie main courses, and we had the 'bebeainetu', a sort of Ethiopian thali, served on an enormous pancake type bread and eaten with fingers. It was delicious – finger licking good in fact. Couscous was spicy, the 'alicha' (fried vegetables) was also moreish, and the whole caboodle came to around a tenner for two of us, with drinks. Heartily recommended.

Café Pushka [£]
16c Market Row, Brixton SW9
0171 738 6161
Transport: Brixton BR/LU
9-5 (except Wed & Sun)
Unlicensed
Counter Service
Smoking
Vegan options

A jolly little veggie caff nicknamed Café Pushchair by locals. Their main courses (we had moist courgette and carrot rissoles with delicious garlic potatoes) come with salad and vegetables, and only cost £4.00. A discount is available to students and UB40 holders. I could have done without the smoking and regret not having tried Pushka's famed hemp seed cake, but I did enjoy its unpretentious charm.

The Jacaranda Garden [£]
11/13 Brixton Station Road, SW9
0171 274 8383
Transport: Brixton BR/LU
Mon-Sat 10.00-7.00
Licensed
Counter/takeaway
Smoking

Stark, bright and stuck on a corner, the Jacaranda is a reliable stand-by whether you've been bargain hunting in Brixton market, or swimming at "The Rec". The food is as eclectic as the clientele and though not specifically vegetarian, there is always a range of interesting meat-free dishes. West African, Jamaican and Creole dishes are on offer, and I had a vegetable gumbo that tasted wonderfully hot and spicy even if the presentation left much to be desired. They also do delicious cakes and a recent addition to the menu is a selection of filled foccacia.

SW10 & 11

Pizza Express [££]
363 Fulham Road, SW10
0171 352 5300
Transport: Fulham Broadway LU
See Kettners on page 53 for further details

Pizza Express [££]
895 Fulham Road, SW10
0171 731 3117
Transport: Putney Bridge LU
See Kettners on page 53 for further details

Pizza Express [££]
230 Lavender Hill, Clapham, SW11
0171 223 5677
Transport: Clapham Junction BR
See Kettners on page 53 for further details

Pizza Express [££]
46 Battersea Bridge Road, SW11
0171 924 2774
Transport: Clapham Junction BR
See Kettners on page 53 for further details

Brixton Market

SW14 & 15

Pizza Express [££]
305 Upper Richmond Road, Roehampton,
SW14
0181 878 6833
Transport: Barnes BR
See Kettners on page [?] for further details

Pizza Express [££]
144 Upper Richmond Road, Putney, SW15
0181 789 1948
Transport: East Putney LU
See Kettners on page [?] for further details

SW16 Streatham

Wholemeal Cafe [£]
1 Shrubbery Road, Streatham, SW16
0181 769 2423
Transport: Streatham BR
7 days Noon - 10
Licensed
Counter service
Non-smoking
Vegan options
Stuck away in a secretive Streatham side
street, Wholemeal was the café I first came
to as a pale Smiths fan, replete with Oscar
Wilde novel, Meat is Murder t-shirt, and my
delicate Smiths-fan girlfriend of the time. It's
still there, in its vege-caff uniform of small
varnished wooden tables, large blackboard
and whitewashed brickwork. Service is
cheerful and the atmosphere relaxed. Lone
diners chow over their newspapers while
lounge Jazz tinkles away in the background.
Regulars seem to come for the respite from
South London hustle and bustle as much as
for the food. Salads are fresh (though they
do use the dreaded iceberg), and on this
visit our Mediterranean Vegetables with
Olives was actually "Mediterranean
Vegetables with Olive". The Banofee Pie
was marvellously sticky, its biscuit base
divine perfection.

SW17 Tooting

Kastoori [£££]
188 Upper Tooting Road, SW17 7EJ
0181 767 7027
Transport: Tooting Broadway LU
Lunch Wed-Sun 12.30-2.30 Dinner 7 days 6-
10.30
Licensed
Table/service
Smoking
Vegan options
Disabled access
In 1972, during Idi Amin's reign of terror in
Uganda, 28 000 Asians were forced to flee
the country for Britain. The majority where
Gujarati Jains who had worked servicing the
British colonial machine. Like many Indian
vegetarian restauranteurs, the Thanki family
came via East Africa, but unlike the others,
they include a taste of East Africa in their
purely veggie menu. The décor is a bit like
your teenage sister's bedroom, all pink and
grey, and the music is best described as
"new age movie soundtrack", but the food
is quite superb. Try the Kasodi (a Swahili
word for corn) with coconut milk and
ground nut sauce, or ask if the green banana
curry is on the menu. Because these dishes
are so popular with local Indians, it may be
wise to ring and book first. Many dishes are
served only on Sundays, the local market
day.

Milan [£]
158 Upper Tooting Road, Tooting, SW17
0181 767 4347
Transport: Tooting Bec/Tooting Broadway LU
7 days 9.30-8
Unlicensed
Counter service
Non-smoking
Vegan options
A small, unobtrusive South Indian sweet
shop and caff. There are a few formica
tables where you can scoff from a
reasonable range of South Indian snacks –
idlis, dosas, and bhel-poori, however you'll
only need to go there if the Kastoori is full.

Sree Krishna [££]
192-194 Tooting High Street, Tooting SW17
0181 672 4250
Transport: Tooting Broadway LU
Mon-Thu 12-3 6-11 Fri-Sat 12-3 6-midnight
Sun 12-3 6-11
Licensed
Table/takeaway service
Smoking
A restaurant with a decent reputation that has remained consistently within the Good Curry Restaurant Guide's Top 100. It's a big one, seating around 120, but the service can be a bit impersonal and the menu, though mostly from the Karala region of South Indian, also has a lot of meat in it. Sree Krishna is a branch of Ragam (see page 56), and seems to suffer from the same pitfalls.

Tumbleweeds [££]
32 Tooting Bec Road, Tooting, SW17
0181 767 9395
Transport: Tooting Bec LU
Tue-Fri 6.30-10.30 Sat-Sun 12-10.30
Licensed
Table service
Non-smoking
Vegan options
Someone went mad with a paint pot at Tumbleweeds. Everything that can be hand-painted, is; walls, chairs, tables, vases, even the windows. Fresh flowers on each table are a nice touch and the music – light, jazzy hip-hop and soul sounds – was the best of any restaurant in the book. There is a limited menu - soup (£2.20), three main courses at £6 a pop. Food is tasty but unimaginative, and a touch expensive for what you get. It's a pity the choice is not greater. I didn't want a main course at lunchtime, and I'd have preferred a sandwich. Serving breakfast might also bring in the punters during the day.

SW18 Wandsworth

Pizza Express [££]
539 Old York Road, Wandsworth, SW18
0181 877 9812
Transport: Wandsworth Town BR
See Kettners on page 53 for further details

SW19 Wimbledon

Good Earth [££££]
81 Ridgeway, Wimbledon SW19
0181 944 8883
Transport: Wimbledon LU/BR
See Good Earth Knightsbridge (page 45) for further details.

Pizza Express [££]
70 Westow Hill, Crystal Palace, SW19
0181 670 1786
Transport: Gypsy Hill/Crystal Palace BR
See Kettners on page 53 for further details

Pierre Lapin [££]
86 The Broadway, Wimbledon, SW19
0181 543 1800
Transport: Wimbledon BR/LU
Mon-Fri 12-3, 6-11 Sat-Sun 12-4, 6-11
Licensed
Table service
Smoking
A bargain choice for veg – head fans of French bistro cooking – slightly saucy, heavy on the stomach and coming in three or four courses. This is a franchise business, but unlike similar operations, the owners have some choice in the bill of fare, and you can expect changes on a regular basis. Fish and seafood are on the menu, but you don't have to worry, as the name suggests Peter Rabbit specialises in vegetable dishes and there are plenty to choose from. If you're a South London herbivore and want a change from the excellent curry houses of Tooting, this could be the place for you.

RESTAURANTS

WEST LONDON

M edia-haunted Soho and the trendy Portobello Road both boast a great variety of veggie-friendly restaurants, cafés and bars. Both areas are eminently walkable, and in neither locality will you be forced against your will to eat yet another omelette. There are African and Indian choices, and in this long thin triangle of London neighbourhoods, a high concentration of new internationally flavoured vegetarian restaurants: The Gate, Blah Blah Blah and Mildred's are all trying, with varying degrees of success, to improve standards and choice.

Books for Cooks provide friendly foodie comfort, and Leith's strive to take the weight off your wallet. All of this within easy reach of trendy young bars, clubs and cinemas. A place to see, be seen, and most importantly, be seen eating good meat-free cuisine.

W1 Mayfair, Soho, Baker Street, Oxford Street

Balans [£££]
60-62 Old Compton Street, Soho, W1
0171 437 5212
Transport: Tottenham Court Road/Leicester
Square LU
Sun-Thu 8-4 Fri-Sat 8-5
Licensed
Table service
Smoking

Approved by a young gay crowd, service can be somewhat robust at this busy Soho coffee bar and restaurant. There's something about being shouted at by a waiter (for sitting in the wrong place) that is slightly off-putting. I was prepared to forgive (though not to tip) because the food was so good. Breakfasts are imaginative, and the majority are veggie, if not vegan. Hash browns come with poached egg and garlicky mushrooms and were hot and peppery, while the blueberry pancakes came with a fruit salad of kiwi, star and passion-fruit. Highly recommended for the cooking and, though not cheap it's money well spent. and worth braving the unpleasant staff.

Cranks [££]
8 Marshall Street, W1V
0171 437 9431
Transport: Oxford Circus LU
Mon-Tue 8-8 Wed-Thu 8-9 Fri 8-8 Sat 9-8
Licensed
Counter/takeaway service
Non-smoking
Vegan options
Disabled access

This branch of London's major vegetarian chain is the flagship of an operation that's been going since 1961, and pioneered veggie cooking in Britain. The name itself should give you an idea of the standing of vegetarians throughout the fifties and sixties. Cranks operate seven restaurants in London, and though opinion seems divided on their merits, I've always found this branch to be of a high quality. This one is a noisy split level canteen where office and shop workers chatter away their lunchtimes with students and cycle messengers. Classical muzak floats in the background, but it makes a change from Bjork and Portishead. The food is rarely thrilling, but is never disappointing. Salads are chock full of interesting leaves, and a main course (I had a warm hearty dish of new potatoes, asparagus and red onions) with two salads, costs £4.95. Their excellent desserts are priced between 95p–£2.00.
Also at: 23 Barrett Street, W1
[0171 495 1340] &
9 Tottenham Street, W1 [0171 631 3912]

Govindas [£]
9-10 Soho Street, W1
0171 437 4928
Transport: Tottenham Court Road LU
Mon-Sat 11-8
Unlicensed
Counter/takeaway service
Non-smoking
Vegan options
Disabled access
Govindas is a big bright canteen situated just off Oxford Street, and owner and operated by Hare Krishna devotees. Your food will be offered to Lord Krishna to bless before cooking. "By eating [the food] one is spiritually benefitted" say the signs "and [eaters] can experience increasing peace of mind and gradual diminishment of material suffering". This is just as well as the cheap all you can eat buffet (dhal, rice, two curries and popadums for a fiver) was both lukewarm and lacking in flavour (though, to be fair, we did turn up just before closing). Notwithstanding that, the atmosphere was friendly and relaxed, staff smiled beatifically, and though we stayed till long after closing time listening to the holy music, no one asked us to leave. More of a cultural than a culinary experience, but for the money you can hardly expect more.

Kettner's [£££]
29 Romilly Street, Soho, W1
0171 734 6112
Transport: Tottenham Court Road/Leicester Square LU
Mon-Sat 11-11
Licensed
Table service
Smoking
Kettner's is part of the Pizza Express empire, though it does its best to disguise the fact. It has all the grandeur of a Viennese dining room, while the prices are not beyond those of the student, and are often cheaper than nearby Soho pasta caffs. A piano tinkles in the background, there is little noise from the rowdies in the bar next

door, and the staff treat both smart and scruffy with the same neglect.

Other outlets in the chain do not have the luxurious intimacy of Kettner's, but are normally clean and sparse, with white table tops and tubular steel seating. The walls sport variations on the Athena modern classic poster, and the music is soft-rock, but the atmosphere is always pleasant and the food uniformly decent.

I've always found Pizza Express to be good value for money, with a decent choice of vegetarian pizza and excellent Peroni beer. The crusts are thin, and the Fiorentina, with egg and spinach, is a firm favourite of mine. Never disappointing but never outstanding.

Mildred's [££]
58 Greek St., Soho, W1V
0171 494 1634
Transport: Tottenham Court Road LU
Mon-Sat 12-11
Licensed
Table/takeaway service
Non-smoking
Vegan options
Disabled access
I make no excuses for raving over Mildred's. Every visit is a pleasure, from the tightly packed blue formica tables which force you to make friends with your neighbours, to the attractive and friendly Colonials who staff the place. When my eating partner asked for her dessert before her main course, our waitress didn't bat an eyelid, and bought us an exciting lemon tart with raspberry coulis and fresh mint. Our main course was pizza with blue cheese, and sundried tomato and basil sausages – imaginative and tasty dishes with excellent textures. The salad was fresh, made with some unusual leaves, and avoided my bête noir, iceberg lettuce. You can also eat outside in the Soho smog, but you'll rarely be disappointed wherever you choose to eat.

Govinda

RESTAURANTS

Minara [£]
I Hanway Place, W I
0171 636 4654
Transport: Tottenham Court Road LU
Lunch 12-3.30 Dinner 5.30-11
Licensed
Table/takeaway service
Smoking
Disabled access
There used to be a fantastic little homemade shrine at the Minara, with Bambi frolicking in a fountain amidst the Hindu deities, but it's gone now. Its absence doesn't seem to have created any more elbow room, and local shop workers jostle for a lunchtime table in this popular restaurant covertly located off Tottenham Court Road. They do great lunchtime deals; an "all you can eat" buffet from £2.95, and various set lunches from £2.50. My vegetable curry was fairly pedestrian, but the kadhi (yoghurt sauce) was memorable, and the pilau buttery and moist. The paratha had a good texture but wasn't oily. Perhaps I was particularly hungry that lunchtime, but the food really did taste wonderful.

Pizza Express
10 Dean Street, Soho W I
0171 437 9595
Transport: Leicester Square/Tottenham Court Road LU
See Kettners on page 53 for further details

Pizza Express
21-22 Barrett Street, W I
0171 629 1001
Transport: Marble Arch LU
See Kettners on page 53 for further details

Pizza Express
29 Wardour Street, W I
0171 437 7215
Transport: Piccadilly Circus LU
See Kettners on page 53 for further details

Pollo [££]
20 Old Compton Street, Soho, W I
0171 734 5917
Transport: Leicester Square LU
Mon-Sat 11.30-11.30
Licensed
Table service
Smoking
There are two types of hipster in London. Those who prefer Pollo, and those who will only eat at nearby Presto. The menu is similar – solid and simple Italian favourites, delivered quickly and cheaply. The finest of fast food, and costing little more than a burger and fries. A meal at Pollo is hardly a comfortable experience, the two small floors heaving with students, budget tourists and the odd celebrity. I once shared a table with Tim Burgess of the Charlatans and Sarah Cracknell of St. Etienne, and it's very unlikely you'll get a table to yourself. There are lots of vegetarian choices, and you can normally convince the waiting staff to submerge your favourite pasta in the sauce of your choice.

Presto [££]
4 Old Compton Street, W I
0171 437 4006
Transport: Leicester Square LU
11.30-11
Licensed
Table service
Smoking
For what it's worth, I much prefer Presto of the Soho pasta joints. For one, I took my future wife there on our first date. The waitresses, then as now, are brusque but motherly, the décor is basic, and the food honest. Derek Jarman (once a regular) beams beatifically from one wall, and the seating is altogether more comfortable than at Pollo. Meat free pasta dishes are plentiful, and if you tell the waitresses exactly what you'd like, they'll usually see what they can do.

Ragam [££]

57 Cleveland Street, W1P 5PQ
0171 636 9098
Transport: Goodge Street/Warren Street LU
Lunch Sun-Mon 12-3
Dinner Sun 6-11 Mon-Thu 6-11.30 Fri 6-12
Sat 6-11.30
Licensed
Table service
Smoking
Vegan options
Disabled access

A small South Indian restaurant which may upset purists as it features a suspiciously large menu of meat dishes, including beef! One can only surmise that this is to keep British diners happy, but I found it rather upsetting, despite the large selection of delicious veggie goodies. Staff are stiff and formal, and the whole place has a kind of shabby, basic quality, but it does serve an area lacking in alternatives.

Shilla [££££]

58 Great Marlborough Street, W1
0171 434 1650
Transport: Oxford Circus LU
Mon-Sat 12-10.30
Licensed
Table service
Smoking

Korean food, despite the ubiquity of Kim chee (pickled cabbage in a chilli sauce), is not ideal for a vegetarian. The best Korean restaurants (normally found not in their home country, but in Hong Kong or Japan) get through more meat than an abattoir, but Shilla do a very reasonable set veggie lunch for about a tenner, and dinner for around twice that. The staff are a bit frosty at times, and the place can get very busy with groups of Japanese tourists, but it's an interesting spot for a birthday night out and a private dining room is available.

The Veeraswamy [££££]

99 Regent Street, W1
0171 734 1401
Transport: Piccadilly Circus LU
Mon-Sat 12-11.30
Licensed
Table service
Smoking

Because of its prime position, and reputation (it is London's oldest Indian restaurant, opened in 1927), Veeraswamy can get very busy with tourists and business-lunchers. It's slightly difficult to see why. The service charge is high (15%), the atmosphere is comfy but dull, and the food ordinary yet expensive. The lunch time buffet (£12.95) does offer a good selection of veggie dishes, as does the separate vegetarian menu, from all over India. Although the staff and presentation are professional and experienced, and despite its consistent Top 100 ranking in the Good Curry Guide, one feels a bit more effort would not go amiss.

Woodlands [££]

77 Marylebone Lane, W1
0171 486 3862
Transport: Bond Street LU
See Woodlands Wembley (page 67) for further details

W2 Paddington, Bayswater, Westbourne Grove

Diwana [££]

50 Westbourne Grove, W2
0171 221 0721
Transport: Bayswater LU
See Diwana Euston on page 35 for further details.

Pizza Express

26 Porchester Road, Westbourne Grove, W2
0171 229 7784
Transport: Royal Oak LU
See Kettner's on page 53 for further details.

Pizza Express
252 Chiswick High Road, Chiswick, W4
0181 747 0193
Transport: Stamford Brook LU
See Kettner's on page 53 for further details.

Pizza Express
23 Bond Street, Ealing, W5
0181 567 7690
Transport: Ealing Broadway LU
See Kettner's on page 53 for further details

W6 Hammersmith

The Gate [£££]
51 Queen Caroline Street, Hammersmith, W6
0181 748 6932
Transport: Hammersmith LU
Mon 6-10.45 Tue-Fri 12-3 6-10.45 Sat 6-10.45
Licensed
Table service
Smoking
Vegan options

Negotiate the church courtyard, and go up the stairs. The Gate is like a big old classroom with a huge portrait of Billie Holiday dominating one wall, and the rear of Hammersmith Odeon glaring at you through the large window. The music is too loud (especially since it was the Housemartins), the food is good, but the portions are small in a well-presented nouveau way. I loved the Sweet Potato Rosti with goat's cheese, which I was reluctantly forced to share with my partner, but I had the Gumbo all to myself, accompanied by refreshing mango chutney. One of London's better veggie restaurants.

W8

Pizza Express
35 Earls Court Road, Earls Court, W8
0171 937 0761
Transport: Earls Court LU
See Kettner's on page 53 for further details

The Gate

W11 Holland Park, Notting Hill

Books for Cooks [££]
4 Blenheim Crescent, W11
0171 221 1992
Transport: Notting Hill Gate/Ladbroke Grove LU
Mon-Sat 9.30-6
Unlicensed BYO
Counter Service
Non-smoking
Vegan options

I couldn't have written this book without the help and encouragement of the lovely staff at Books for Cooks. If you want to know what Elvis ate in the Army or need to devise a diet for an Italian Series A footballer, this is the place to go. There is also a small café counter at the back where the best recipes from their books are tried out. Normally one dish will be suitable for veggies, and it is bound to be superior to most meat-free fare. Cooks work on a rota but my favourite, Jennifer Joyce, dished up a superlative chick-pea salad with tasty greens, and Provençal Grilled Vegetables that were both healthy and full of flavour. The emphasis is on freshness and immediacy. As you'd expect from one of London's secret gastronomic delights, a table is not always easy to come by at the weekend.

Leith's [££££]
92 Kensington Park Road, W11
0171 229 4481
Transport: Notting Hill Gate LU
7 days 7.30-11.30
Licensed
Table service
Smoking
Vegan options

One feels one should be wary of Leith's. The famous school is now a separate concern, the catering business has been sold off to a French mega-companie retaining only the name, and the sandwich bars at the Natural History and Design Museums promise much, but deliver little. Fortunately Prue keeps an interest in the restaurant, which is as reassuringly expensive and snooty as ever. An oasis of quiet and comfort, one sinks into deep upholstery and warms up the credit card. Food is Modern British, which can mean Puy lentils and Mediterranean vegetables. Thankfully, Leith's love veggies, and there is a marvellous fixed price vegetarian menu - imaginative, mouthwatering and slightly cheaper than the meaty menu. Service is old fashioned and very polite, as you'd expect.

Mandola Café [££]
139 Westbourne Grove, W11
0171 229 4734
Transport: Notting Hill Gate LU
Mon-Sat 12-11.30
Unlicensed
Counter/Takeaway service

A small Sudanese restaurant with simple furnishings and walls hung with shields, drums and gourds. The food is simple too and you'll be reminded of Middle-Eastern food, although the use of peanuts is common in African cooking. There is a good range of salads and vegetarian dishes, mostly based on pulses of various sorts. Try anything with plump juicy broad beans – delicious!

Pizza Express
137 Notting Hill Gate, Notting Hill, W11
0171 229 6000
Transport: Notting Hill LU
See Kettner's on page 53 for further details.

Pizza Express
7 Rockley Road, Shepherds Bush, W11
0181 749 8582
Transport: Shepherds Bush LU
See Kettner's on page 53 for further details.

W12 Shepherds Bush

Blah Blah Blah [£££]
78 Goldhawk Road, Shepherd's Bush, W12
0181 746 1337
Transport: Goldhawk Road LU
Mon-Sat 12-3 7.30-11
Unlicensed BYO
Table service
Smoking
Vegan options
Wacky décor – trees and anti-aircraft lights!
The music is loud too. Loud music is always
for the benefit of the staff, not the customer,
and the volume was high enough for us to
ask for it to be turned down. Friends have
raved about Blah Blah Blah for years, but I
was disappointed. I hope it was a bad night.
Service was over familiar and verging on
insolent, the Bubble and Squeak was more
like mash (though the piccalilly was quite
wonderful), and the nouvelle cuisine style
presentation meant that portions were
small. A regular tells me that when the boss
is away standards fall and on the evidence of
my visit, although the food was interesting, it
was not worth the money.

Books for Cooks

WEST CENTRAL LONDON

The most walkable of all the districts in this book, and with a wide choice for veggies, the WC postal codes take in Theatre – and Cinema – land, Covent Garden, Bloomsbury and the Strand. In short, the areas visited most often by night-lifers and tourists. In this respect it offers wonderful choice for budget eaters (Gaby's, LSE), for those with a taste for the exotic (Calabash or Wagamama), or the Bohemian in search of endangered coffee bar life (Bunjies).

Cranks has three outlets in the area, and there is of course the execrable Neal's Yard – an amalgam of tasteless and unimaginative vegetarian caffs, catering to a sure supply of young tourists to whom they do a great disservice. No wonder it's so difficult to get a seat in Food For Thought – it's full of refugees from the Yard around the corner.

On the whole the area is one in which it's easy for the unsuspecting to be taken advantage of. Tourists make an easy target for those wanting to make a fast buck, and this goes for vegetarian tourists as much as meat eaters. It's up to you to put these people out of business by refusing to accept second rate food and sloppy service.

WC1 Russell Square, Bloomsbury

The Greenhouse [££]
16 Chenies Street, Bloomsbury, WC1
0171 637 8038
Transport: Goodge Street LU
Mon 10-10 (women only 8-10) Tue-Fri 10-10
Sat 12-10
Unlicensed
Counter/takeaway service
Non-smoking
Vegan options
Unless I misheard, the Greenhouse is favourite hang out for thespians. It's a basement café beneath the Drill Hall theatre, and it's sometimes hard to get a table, making it claustrophobic if you do. The food tastes pretty good, but the choices are unsurprising – your usual veggie stews, soups, salads and quiches. Still, it's not expensive, obviously has its regulars and seems terribly popular.

Pizza Express
30 Coptic Street, WC1
0171 636 3232
Transport: Holborn LU
See Kettner's on page 53 for further details.

Wagamama [££]
4 Streatham Street, off Bloomsbury Street, WC1
0171 323 9223
Transport: Tottenham Court Road LU
Mon-Fri 12-2.30 6-11 Sat 1.30-3 6-11
Licensed
Table service
Non-smoking
Vegan options
The first thing you'll notice is the length of the queue outside this popular Japanese noodle bar, but don't let that put you off as it moves quickly and efficient waiters will order you drinks, while you wait. Once seated you'll be fed pretty swiftly and it is always worth the wait. This basement restaurant is cavernous, the long shared benches a modern blond. Everything is well designed – the waiters' t-shirts by Paul Smith to the nifty computerised note pads that whisk your order to the kitchen. The food is good, simple and noodly, and I recommend both the raw salad and the raw juice, which will have the goodness coursing through your veins in seconds. There are fish dishes, but more than enough choices for veg-heads and despite the high quality of the staff, the food and the surroundings, you won't be out of pocket.

Wagamama

WC2 Covent Garden, Strand, Leicester Square

Bunjies [£]

27 Lichfield Street, WC2H 9NI
0171 240 1796
Transport: Covent Garden/Leicester Square LU
Mon-Sat 12-11
Licensed
Counter Service
Smoking
Vegan options

"London's Folk Singing Centre and Vegetarian Restaurant" has been a bohemian basement for over forty years, and musicians of the calibre of David Bowie, and Simon and Garfunkel, and comedians from Eddie Izzard to Newman and Baddiel have all appeared in its dingy cellars. It is a great place to wallow in fifties coffee bar nostalgia, perhaps the last of its kind. Unfortunatley, the food also harks back to the fifties – it's cheap, but pretty inedible. Best to visit for a coffee or tea in a meat-free atmosphere of goateed poets scribbling in notebooks, or pale existential girls in black tights reading battered Penguin paperbacks.

Calabash [£££]

The Africa Centre, 38 King Street, WC2E
0171 836 1976
Transport: Covent Garden LU
Mon-Sat 5.30-11
Licensed
Table service
Smoking

Tucked away in the basement of the Africa Centre, the Calabash offers superb African cuisine from all corners of this vast continent. The staff are friendly and helpful, the glasses and teapots polished to perfection, and warm African colours and sounds soothe you into the menu. It offers at least five or six vegetarian starters and main courses. The spicy stews make generous use of groundnut sauces, and there is a choice of rice, ground rice or yam

with every dish. Portions are big, but easily washed down with beers from Zimbabwe or Namibia. Topped off with Abbysinian coffee on a burning pot of frankincense, it's a unique experience and vegetarians are well served.

Cranks [££]

8 Adelaide Street, WC2
0171 836 0660
Transport: Charing Cross BR/LU
See Cranks on page 52 for further details

Cranks [££]

1 The Market, Covent Garden, WC2
0171 379 6508
Transport: Covent Garden LU
See Cranks on page 52 for further details.

Cranks [££]

17 Great Newport Street, WC2
0171 836 5226
Transport: Leicester Square LU
See Cranks on page 52 for further details.

First Out [££]

52 St. Giles High Street, WC2
0171 240 8042
Tottenham Court Road LU
Mon-Sat 11-11.15 Sun 2-7
Licensed
Counter service
Smoking
Vegan options

In the shadow of Centrepoint, First Out is a handily situated, user friendly vegetarian lesbian and gay coffee bar. A great meeting place, First Out is also a good stopping off point for information about what's on – the floor by the door is habitually knee deep in flyers and free newspapers. Cakes are healthy, the staff cute, and the walls are normally home to the work of young and exciting unknown artists.

Food For Thought [£]

31 Neal Street, Covent Garden, WC2H 9PR
0171 836 9072
Transport: Covent Garden LU
Mon-Sat 9.30-8.00 Sun 10.30-4.00
Unlicensed
Counter service
Non-smoking
Vegan options

Food for Thought is undoubtedly the best of the Covent Garden veggie eateries. It's like a little sixties throwback, with hints of Scandinavian wholesomeness and a touch of the Terence Conran's (though slightly down at heel). The crowded basement is invariably noisy and stuffy in summer, and the packed bench seating leads to Food for Thought's biggest drawback – the difficulty in finding somewhere to sit. Although FFT is exactly what you'd expect from a vegetarian eating experience and pulls no surprises, it does do its thing very well, and I would recommend it – if you can get a seat.

Gaby's Continental Bar [£]

30 Charing Cross Road, WC2
0171 839 4233
Transport: Leicester Square LU
7 days 9-Midnight
Licensed
Table/counter/takeaway service
Smoking
Vegan options
Disabled access

Gaby's is a favourite of all sorts of West End detritus; bookish types with Proust, tourists looking for a taste of home, cinema, theatre and concert goers. I used to hang out here before a gig at the Marquee or Astoria, when it wasn't worth going home after work. Established in 1965, Gaby's serve an eclectic mix of Jewish, Middle-Eastern, and "Continental" food (whatever that is). It sells some of the best salt beef and pastrami in London apparently, but if you're not put off by that, drop in for their crispy falafel or honey drenched, nutty baklava. Also on the menu are vegetarian couscous, mousaka and lasagne which while not up to the standard of their falafel, are a welcome change from the lentil-mania of many "proper" veggie eateries in the area. They also have the most interesting takeaway salad bar in the area with a dazzling array of unusual looking Middle-Eastern choices.

The Café [£]

London School Of Economics, Houghton Street, WC2
0171 405 7686
Transport: Holborn LU
Mon-Fri 9-5
Unlicensed
Counter service
Non-smoking
Vegan options
Disabled access

The Café is so cheap you can't expect haute cuisine, but for inexpensive and filling stodge it's a useful stop off in the centre of town. The days of student radicalism at the LSE are pretty much over and although there are still political posters and paper sellers aplenty, most of the walls shout health advice – more a testament to students' sexual proclivities and drug taking habits than their political awareness. With a multi-cultural mix of students, food crosses barriers. The soup (on my visit it was Tomato and Tarragon – 75p) is usually good. Main courses (£1.80) come in large portions and my Cassoulet was at least hot and filling. Pride of place goes to a certificate for "Best Improvement in percentage of plastic cups recycled 1992".

RESTAURANTS

Neal's Yard Bakery Co-operative and Tea Room [££]

6 Neal's Yard, WC2H
0171 836 5199
Transport: Covent Garden LU
Mon-Sat 10.30-5.00
Unlicensed
Counter service
Non-smoking
Vegan options

The popularity of this location means that places like Neal's Yard Bakery and Tea Room don't have to make much of an effort. Their range of bread and cakes use 100% organic flour, no refined sugar and filtered water, but these are the usual mushy wholefoods that vegetarians have had to put up with for so long. You can take-away or eat in the upstairs dining area. I went late in the afternoon, and obviously interrupted the chatting staff. "Can I ask a couple of questions?" I said, wanting to know something about the menu. My waitress raised her eyebrows, sighed and groaned "Go on then". I left feeling as reluctant to be there as she obviously did.

Vegetarian Cuisine

Jubilee Market Hall, Covent Garden, WC2
0171 497 0088
Transport: Covent Garden LU
7 Days 8-6
Unlicensed
Counter service
Smoking

One hardly expects to discover high quality vegetarian food on the "Fast Food Deck" of the bustling Jubilee Hall, and this stand-up caff, situated next door to the London Transport Museum, is pretty pedestrian. Large portions of microwaved veggie nosh (including, disastrously, a stir-fry) are served with plastic cutlery. Salads are pale and dependent on iceberg lettuce. Vegetarian Cuisine is notable, however, for providing a delivery service for local businesses, so those who cannot leave their market stalls and offices can still eat.

World Food Café [££]

14 Neal's Yard, WC2H
0171 379 0298
Transport: Covent Garden LU
Sun-Tue 12.00-5.00 Wed-Fri 12.00-7.30
Licensed
Counter service
Non-smoking
Vegan options

A light, airy, first floor dining room overlooking less interesting establishments in Neal's Yard. The friendly staff flit about busily, and serve up tasty portions of food inspired by international travel. On the menu you'll usually find an Indian dish, something from Africa and perhaps something Mexican or Turkish, with big plates of interesting salads. All main meals clock in at around six quid, and you are unlikely to be disappointed as the management and staff here really do seem to care about giving you good wholesome meat-free food.

Paprika Vegetarian Restaurant [£]

Neal's Yard, WC2H
Transport: Covent Garden LU
7 Days 12-7
Licensed
Counter service
Smoking
Vegan options
Disabled access

The Paprika is a relative newcomer to Neal's Yard, with a bright, colourful exterior and an interior that looks suspiciously like a jazzed-up ice cream parlour. This gives it a gay informality that is a nice change from the over-designed 'simplicity' of some veggie caffs. Not only are most of Paprika's meals vegan, but they are also salt, sugar and oil free. According to a blackboard outside, they are also (somewhat mysteriously) "suitable for children". At £4.00 for three courses, it won't bankrupt their parents either.

OUTER LONDON

The London postal codes give us a false idea of what lies within the boundaries of our city, whereby Merton and Mill Hill are in London, but Wembley isn't. There are miles upon miles of London with 0181 telephone numbers which as far as the Royal Mail are concerned do not belong to London.

Vegetarians should ignore the peculiarities of the Post Office and parcel themselves off to Wembley, Southall or Rayners Lane, for here is to be found very good Indian food at bargain prices. A tube trip to the end of the Piccadilly line will bring you to one of the most exciting fast food eating experiences in London, where the food is cooked fresh before your eyes and brought sizzling to your table at Balti Hut.

Wembley, home to much of London's Gujurati community, is always a curry hot spot, as is Southall, where every second shop front conceals a restaurant where the local Punjabi and Pakistani gourmands chow down.

'A' Sweet [£]

106 The Broadway, Southall, UB1
0181 574 2821
Transport: Southall BR
Opening Hours
Unlicensed
Counter/takeaway service
Smoking
Disabled access

The red and white livery of this popular South Indian café announces that it was established in 1970. It's not particularly friendly but the locals obviously enjoy using the place and as Southall has a high concentration of Punjabi restaurants, karahi and kebab shops, 'A' Sweet's "hot snacks, meals and sweets" may be your only vegetarian option.

Balti Hut [££]

435 Alexandra Avenue, Rayners Lane, HA2
0181 868 0007
Transport: Rayners Lane LU
7 days 12-11
Unlicensed
Table/takeaway service
Smoking
Vegan options

Many is the sub-standard curry house that has suddenly styled itself 'balti'. A balti is a small iron wok, but many restaurants have taken to slopping your grub into a balti (aka 'a karahi') before serving, regardless of how they cook it. Not so the Balti Hut, which cooks your order in an open plan kitchen and brings it to your table with smiles, advice and suggestions. As the name intimates, Balti Hut is trying a fast food approach. The radio pumps up the bhangra, and the tables are wipe clean formica. But this is no quick profit chain. The food tastes fantastic, dazzling the tongue and nose with flavours, and if you've been to a Brick Lane balti-house, you'll find this stuff unrecognisably superior.

Chetna's [££]
420 High Road, Wembley HA9
0181 900 1466
Transport: Wembley Park/Wembley Central LU
Opening Hours: Tue-Fri 12-3 6-10.30 Sat-Sun
1-10.30
Unlicensed
Table service
Smoking
Vegan options
Disabled access
A large and frequently packed bhel-poori house, extremely popular with the local Gujarati population who queue to get in. The stencilled signs and lack of polish may put some off, and the menu holds few surprises, but it obviously has plenty going for it.

Hockney's [£££]
98 High Street, Croydon CR0
0181 688 2899
Transport: East/West Croydon BR
Mon 10.30-2.30 Tue-Sat 10.30-5.30
Unlicensed
Counter service
No smoking
Vegan options
Hockney's, part of a Buddhist run health food store, is one of those cafe's where you'll get a seat at any time except lunchtime, when it's heaving with sweaty suited types. Staff are unfailingly friendly and helpful, and the restaurant clean and smart, though it lacks a bit of character. The menu stays much the same from day to day – soups, salads, baked spuds and a few main courses.

Rajbhog [£]
140 Ealing Road, Wembley, HA9
0181 903 9395
Transport: Alperton/Wembley Central LU
Mon-Fri 11-10 Sat-Sun 11-11
Unlicensed
Table service
Smoking
A large and very popular restaurant, not too far from the Western International market, and serving up specialities from South India, Bombay and the Punjab. There are some odd dishes on the menu, which make Rajbhog one of the more eccentric restaurant choices – for instance the chat may come with chips and some dishes are served with white bread. Still, that probably means it's only too authentic, and the clientele are are 75% Indian. Their dosas and idlis are not only good value for money, they taste excellent too. Worth exploring.

Rani [£££]
3 Hill Street, Richmond, Surrey TW9
0181 332 2322
Transport: Richmond BR/LU
See Rani East Finchley on page 33 for details.

Woodlands [£££]
402 High Street, Wembley, HA9
0181 902 9869
Transport: Wembley Central LU
7 days 12-2.30 6-10.30
Licensed
Table service
Non-smoking
Vegan options
Disabled access
The Woodlands décor is as crisp as neighbouring Chetna's is shabby. But it's never as full and Woodlands has a variable reputation with the eaters of Wembley. Their food is edible enough, but never goes out of its way to dazzle, and you get the feeling there's a lack of love for what they do. Woodlands is part of a chain however, and this may explain why the food here is so unimpressive.

RESTAURANTS

SHOPPING

Spitalfields Market

HIGH STREET CHAINS

NOP research found that seven out of ten Londoners believed that there would be less meat eaten in the future and more vegetarians. Perhaps it's not surprising therefore that the high street chains have begun to cater, to varying degrees, for their meat-free customers. At the end of the day it is normally more convenient, and certainly cheaper, for vegetarians to shop at supermarket chains than at wholefood stores.

Chains not included here were either unable or unwilling to help, but were in any case the smaller strings of supermarkets. Their approach to customer information and public relations probably means that they will remain so, for vegetarian or not, people want to know what they are eating, especially with food scares lurking around every aisle.

Stores such as Tesco have in fact gone out of their way to forge links with the Vegetarian Society, and while some may see this as opportunism, it is really just good business sense. Never forget that the first duty of any business is to its shareholders. The customer always comes second unless their concerns coincide. The fact that they often do points to a massive shift in society away from meat eating (particularly red meat), and the emergence of a more knowledgeable shopper....Keep up the pressure.

SHOPPING

SAINSBURY'S

Sainsbury's have just over 80 stores in the Greater London area, and have concentrated their approach to vegetarian and vegan customers on clear labelling of food products. Non-meat eaters can also request their 34 page guide, "Vegetarians & Vegans: A Product Guide for Special Dietary requirements". This lists non-meat choices section by section, so that you'll know whether the deli counter American Style Potato Salad really is veggie. It also lists vegetarian cosmetics and toiletries, and I found their approach to the issue the best of all the chains.

Sainsbury's sell over twenty veggie sandwiches, and more than fifty meat free ready meals.

WAITROSE

Waitrose are one of my favourite supermarkets. Their wholenut peanut butter uses apple juice rather than sugar as a sweetener, and their malted grain granary bread is still the business as far as I'm concerned. Waitrose sent me a list of over two and a half thousand meat-free products, but this list did include tea, fruit and rice etc.

Nonetheless, there are a good selection of vegetarian sandwiches and ready meals, though there are relatively few Waitrose stores in capital (only ten, as opposed to over 40 Sainsbury's) so they may not be the handiest choice for Londoners.

TESCO

Tesco stock over 1500 products which are suitable for vegetarians, (i.e. free from animal products and by-products with the exception of eggs, milk products and honey, and free of by-products of the fishing industry). All vegetarian foods are labelled with the three-leaf "Suitable for Vegetarians" symbol, which was introduced as far back as 1985 in response to customer demand.

Vegetarian customers can request a leaflet in any store, detailing veggie choices for snacks, lunches, and ready meals, or a list of the full range of products. Tesco also plans to publish a list of foods suitable for vegans.

BOOTS

There's a Boots the Chemist on nearly every high street and they've started to sell lunchtime snacks over the past few years, some of which are rather good. Ignoring their SHAPERS range and the dubious morality of diet foods, Boots sell around twenty veggie sandwiches, ten meat-free pies and pasties, and three pre-packed salads. One or two of their selections are rather bland, normally the ones dependent on cheese, but their Bombay Potato Flatbread, and the Mozzarella Foccacia are highly palatable. Vegetarian and vegan foods are labelled accordingly.

PRET A MANGER

Prêt à Manger have been building a growing reputation in the high streets of Central London, with their distinctive chrome furniture, bandana headed staff and great sandwiches. Every week a new store seems to open (there were, at the time of writing, 32 in the London postal area). Prêt offer a range of around ten sandwiches suitable for vegetarians, all of them on interesting breads (i.e. Walnut, or Marbled Tomato), and contain plenty of fresh vegetables and salad leaves.

During the winter they sell soups at their outlets, all of which are vegetarian (except at their branch in the National Gallery which sells Smoked Haddock!).

Prêt tell me they are "constantly looking to increase the amount of vegetarian products that we sell" and in the near future will be introducing a Noodle Salad, a new Vegetarian Sushi, and a Cream Cheese sandwich with Roasted Vegetables.

FAST FOOD

With all the options in this book I hope you'll never have to eat in a faceless multi-national fast food chain. It's the small guys that need and deserve your money, and who really serve your needs. At the same time, it is a measure of our spending power and growing numbers that burger bars like MacDonalds have finally introduced a vege-burger. Should your children eventually succumb to peer pressure, and, despite the good food you've always brought them up on, drag you into the formica nightmare zone, make sure you stick to the following.

BURGER KING

For £1.86 the Spicy Beanburger isn't too bad a deal and, although it's been on the menu for over ten years, is still a popular choice in their 35 restaurants. It comes in a soft sesame bun, oval shaped and cut in half, with two slices of processed cheese, ketchup and fresh tomato. The burger itself is slightly spicy with a tang of chilli, but without any subtlety. It contains kidney beans and carrots, has good flavour, and is the best of the high street burgers.

MACDONALDS

There are over 60 MacDonalds outlets in London. Their speciality is the Vegetable Deluxe (£1.74), a thin, crispy burger which is hard to taste through all the mayonnaise. This is garnished with tomato and iceberg lettuce and slipped between the halves of a soft sesame bun. Quite filling, unmemorable and not unpleasant.

MAIL ORDER

Alara Wholefoods

110-112 Camley Street, London NW1 0PF
0171 387 9303

Alara stock a huge range of wholefood products, from beans, cereals, dried fruits and flour, to nuts, cordials and organic baby food. They also offer a pre-packed range of foods (muesli, sundried fruit and veg, and various Bombay Mix type snacks), with many lines in two or three different pack sizes. The minimum order for delivery within the M25 is £150, but I daresay you could make a smaller order if you collect. The people at Alara – who also run a splendid shop in Marchmont Street (see page 76) – are very friendly and committed, and will help you find exactly what you're looking for.

Roselyne Masselin's Fresh & Frozen Foods

18 Belmont Court, Belmont Hill, St. Albans, Herts. AL1 1RB
01272 837643
Vegan options

Ros has produced a range of her favourite veggie meals which, frozen in one portion foil containers, are highly suitable for those of us spending a lot of time in front of the TV. Most are vegan, but sound mouthwatering enough, with dishes like Mushroom and Black Eyed Bean Curry, or Courgette and Almond Raised Pie. Single portions are priced at £1.80, and a minimum order is £15.00 though delivery is free. What a great idea.

Traidcraft plc.

Kingsway, Gateshead,
Tyne & Wear, NE11 0NE
0191 491 0855

Traidcraft aim to build a better world by establishing long-term trading partnerships with people in developing countries and ensuring that a fair price is paid for products and labour. These relationships help improve working conditions, and bring workers into the decision making process. Prices are good, as should your karma be when you purchase their products. Tea, coffee and cocoa are the most obvious commodities, but there is also jam from Burkina Faso (Africa's poorest country), honey from Latin America, nut spreads, sugar, chocolate, rice and breakfast cereals. Give Traidcraft a go – it's a real opportunity to make a difference.

Vegetarian Express

Unit 46, WENTA Business Centre, Colne Way, Watford, Herts. WD2 4ND
01923 249714

Apart from the usual array of wholefood provisions, Vegetarian Express supply a range of Japanese products and sea vegetables, and ready 'gourmet' veggie meals for the catering industry. These include Mexican Enchiladas, Cauliflower and Chick Pea Korma, Chimichanga and Moussaka. As Vegetarian Express supply many of the flans, pies, filo parcels and salads that you'll eat in your local veggie caff or wholefood store, you may well have tasted their fare already.

Organic Express

0181 694 2220

Organic Express are a new company based in South East London and are operating a novel 'box' scheme. For £8 you can purchase a large box of organic veg (£4 for a box of fruit) which is delivered to your door. It seems like a good idea, and the onus is obviously on the company to make sure your box is of a high quality. You can also buy your own choice of produce, wholefoods and environmentally friendly household products from their list but, as they are new, the selection at the moment is limited.

Alara Wholefoods

WHOLEFOOD STORES

There are many wholefood stores in London but, perhaps surprisingly, the word 'wholefood' does not equal 'vegetarian'. Wholefood stores are often better places to buy patchouli oil than a good veggie snack, and seem unable to grasp that many vegetarians aren't interested in wearing tie-dye t-shirts. There are exceptions however. Maida Vale's Realfood Store, for instance, is an inspiration, offering delicious high quality food that is meat free in a beautifully designed atmosphere which is centuries away from the scuffed wooden floorboards and surly staff of many smaller stores, and the sterility of unimaginative high street wholefood chains.

The stores included here are either those which offer something special, or those which come highly recommended, even if I found they didn't live up to their billing.

East

Friends
83 Roman Road, Bethnal Green, E2
0181 980 1843
Transport: Bethnal Green LU
Mon-Sat 9.30-6 Thu 9.30-4 Fri 9.30-7
Like the nearby Cherry Orchard restaurant, Friends is run co-operatively by Buddhists from the local Buddhist centre. The usual veggie shop staples are in evidence, and there are a range of lunchtime snacks and pies etc. No fresh organic fruit and vegetables appeared to be on offer though.

Spitalfields Market
Commercial Street, E1
Transport: Liverpool Street LU
Mon-Sun 9-6 (shops) Sun 11-3 (market)
A five acre undercover site just around the corner from Brick Lane that used to be home to a large fruit, veg and flower market. There is a wide choice of shops and stalls selling Camden-style handicrafts and essential oils etc., but it's also an excellent spot to pick up organic produce, bread and cakes, and such oddities as carrot juice, tofu and hemp seed. Like an enormous wholefood supermarket, but with much more besides.

East Central

Freshlands Health Store
196 Old Street, EC1V
0171 250 1708
Transport: Old Street LU
Mon-Fri 10.30-6.30 Sat 10.30-4.30
Starting as a small wholefood shop in 1977, Freshlands is now situated on two floors, the ground featuring the usual dried and prepared veggie foods, as well as a salad bar and soup kettle popular with local office workers. The basement houses the homeopathic and aromatherapy side of the business which has now become what they call a 'healthcare practice'. Freshlands also produce a quarterly newsletter with recipes and nutrition information.

North

Green Earth Wholefoods
49 Stoke Newington Church Street, Stoke Newington, N16
0171 923 1477
Transport: Stoke Newington BR
Mon-Thu 9.30-6 Fri 9.30-7 Sat 10-7
There doesn't seem to be a whole lot of food in this wholefood store, though they do sell Cranks breads. Plenty of dippy hippy paraphernalia, festival wear, incense and aromatherapy gubbins.

North West

Sesame

128 Regents Park Road, Primrose Hill, NW1
0171 586 3779
Transport: Chalk Farm BR/LU
Mon-Sat 10-6 Sun 12-5
Sesame is situated in one of my favourite parts of London, home to Engels, Sylvia Plath, and 101 Dalmations. It's been open for around a quarter century, and has a cheerful window of vegetables and boxes of seaweeds. At the back a beautiful stained glass window lets in light from the garden. You can pick up good lunchtime pastas and soups here, but sadly staff here are amongst the most unhelpful I've come across. Their boredom and reluctance to help spoils what is otherwise a wonderful local store.

South East

Baldwins Health Store

171 Walworth Road, SE17
0171 701 4892
Transport: Elephant & Castle BR/LU
Mon-Sat 9.00-5.30
Situated next door to Baldwin's traditional apothecary, which promises "Herbs, Roots, Barks, Gums, Waxes and Incense" the Health Store doesn't have a huge choice of vegetarian food, just run of the mill takeaway standbys and dried pastas and rices. Like its next door neighbour it has a wide range of homeopathic remedies, tinctures, compounds, and vitamins. Staff are rather brusque and hassled looking, but it is always busy.

Coopers Natural Foods

17 Lower Marsh, SE1
0171 261 9314
Transport: Waterloo BR/Lambeth North LU
Mon-Fri 8.30-5.30 Sat 10-12.30
Green paint, well-trodden floorboards - Coopers looks like it's been around since Lower Marsh was a bog, but in fact it has only been there for fifteen years. The staff are approachable, the store is simply laid out, and there is a better choice of tea than I have seen anywhere. A very big sweetie bar too, as good as any newsagents. Heavily used by the local market traders, its excellent take-away service includes fresh coffee, soup, sandwiches, delicious pizzas and quiches.

South West

Balham Wholefood & Health Store

8 Bedford Hill, Balham, SW12
0181 673 4842
Mon-Sat 9.30-6 Tue-Thu 9.30-7
A tiny, fragrant store, literally packed to the rafters with wholefood goodies. It's a bit of a squeeze getting round the aisles, and there isn't much in the way of fresh food or snacks, but there's little else in this part of the South London. For such a small shop, it manages to fit in a surprisingly good book section.

Brixton Wholefoods

59 Atlantic Road, Brixton, SW9
0171 737 2210
Transport: Brixton BR/LU
Tue/Wed/Thu/Sat 9.30-5.30 Mon/Fri 9.30-6
Under a rumbling railway arch in the back end of Brixton, this diminutive store is a friendly meeting place for all manner of Brixtonians, and judging by the ads and messages in the windows, an important information point. Inside are sweetie jars full of teas, herbs and spices, and shelves of fresh breads, glorious green spinach and free-range eggs. The store does good takeaway foods and snacks. The pizza is delicious, as are the tofu and mushroom pies, and the cakes are moist and inviting.

SHOPPING

West Central

Alara Wholefoods
58/60 Marchmont Street, WC1
T: 0171 837 1172
F: 0171 833 8089
Transport: Russell Square LU
Mon-Fri 9-7 Sat 10-6
Alara is a lesson in how it should be done, and no wonder – owner Chiara has had 13 years in her Marchmont St. one-stop shop to get it right. Outside is a table full of fresh herbs and organic fruit and veg. Inside amidst the dried grains and Ecover, there is a super salad bar (including one salad with seaweed, a relative rarity) and you can buy a bottle of "hangover free" organic wine to wash it down with. Alara also do their own baking and their pizza, quiches and pies are all vegan; in their spare time they are one of the largest manufacturers of muesli in the country.

Neal's Yard Wholefood Warehouse
21-23 Shorts Gardens, WC2
0171 836 5151
Transport: Covent Garden LU
Mon-Fri 9-7 Sat 9-6.30 Sun 11-5.30
Despite its flagship position on the entrance to Neal's Yard, this well-disguised Holland and Barrett branch is a disappointment. It is rather small, and lacks the character of a Coopers or Alara. All the usual grains, cheeses and dried fruits, but the breads are not sugar free, and there seems little real attention paid to any philosophy of healthy eating.

West

Realfood Store
14 Clifton Road, Maida Vale, W9
0171 266 1162
Transport: Warwick Avenue LU
Mon-Fri 8.30-7.45 Sat 8.30-6
Although technically a wholefood store, you'll feel like you've stumbled into a Conran restaurant when you visit Realfood.

The design is crisp and clean, well laid out with plenty of space for the eye to take in the top quality victuals. The staff are welcoming and cheerful without being sloppy, and there is a fine kitchen counter for delicious take home foods – soups, sandwiches and some of the most interesting salads I've seen. Not just a veggie pleasure, but a joy for any foodie. If only they were all as good as Realfood.

Wholefood Organics
24 Paddington Street, London W1
0171 935 3924
Transport: Baker Street LU
Mon-Thu 8.45-6 Fri 8.45-6.30 Sat 8.45-1
Wholefood was founded in 1960 by members of the Organic Soil Association, and is now a wholly owned subsidiary of the Wholefood Charitable Trust. It has a devout and slightly neglected feeling, tucked away on a quiet street. Purists may be put off by Wholefood's connection to a small organic butchers shop along the road, but there is a reasonable selection of organic fruit and veg, a good choice of organic wines, and an extensive bookshop, which claims to have "the widest selection in the country", though I very much doubt it.

Wild Oats
210 Westbourne Grove, W11
0171 229 1063
Transport: Bayswater LU
Mon 9-7 Tue 10-7 Wed-Fri 9-7 Sat 9-6 Sun 10-5
A superior and roomy wholefood store on three levels. Nicely laid out and decorated with large enamel advertising signs on the walls, and a veritable supermarket of everything from fruit bars to wines and oils. Particularly impressive is the basement with its selection of Japanese foods, and the organic produce is fresh and plump with goodness and flavour.

Planet Organic
42 Westbourne Grove
London W2 5FH
0171 221 7171
Transport: Royal Oak/Bayswater LU
Mon-Sat 9-8 Sun 11-5
A surprisingly big store considering the small shop front. Inside is London's best organic selection. Fruit, flowers, veg., grains, wine and cheese, and though not exclusively veggie (there is a large selection of organic meat and fish) their non-meat products are as good as you'll find in the capital. If you think there is something quite un-English about the bright approach of Planet Organic, you'd be right. The store (and it is a 'store', not a 'shop') is owned and managed by two Americans; Renee Elliot and Jonathan Dwek. They are introducing some of the best things about shopping over there, over here. Try the juice bar for a pep up after the stress of fighting your way through Portobello Road market.

SHOPPING

EXTRAS

ALCOHOL

EXTRAS

The pub is a dangerous place for the vegetarian (and indeed for animals). Before bottling, wine is 'cleared' using gelatine, isinglass (fish bladders), eggs or dried blood, and milk. Isinglass is also used in similar processes in bitter beer, particularly 'real ale' and Guinness. Spirits are okay on the whole, though some liqueurs and fancy fashionable concoctions (you'll know these by the silly 'sophisticated' name) are dodgy.

For beer you should stick to lagers, though if you really want to make a stand against brewers using animal products, drink the German or Czech varieties, all of which are brewed in accordance with strict laws hundreds of years old to ensure the ingredients never vary. The Czech's drink more beer than anyone else and expect the best, so you could do worse than go with them.

I'm told the Vegetarian Wine Club (see Organisations p.   ) are still around to sell vegetarian wines by mail order, but my attempts to contact them have failed. The Soil Association (86 Colston Street, Bristol, BS1 5BB) are an organisation committed to the propagation of organic farming methods, and can advise on organic wines which are vegetarian.

For those who "like bitter", but aren't willing to compromise, I suggest you put the breweries under pressure. If vegetarians can change the way the major supermarkets do business, we can do the same with the big beer brewers.

CATERERS

used to deal with caterers on an almost daily basis, and they can all provide vegetarian food. Catering, however, can be expensive, and very few deliver outstanding imagination and creativity to the table. Those that do – rightly I think – cause more stress in the wallet region. Therefore it follows that the production of high quality carrotty canapés and flesh-free fork buffets will put you out of pocket. My advice is to ask your favourite veggie restauranteur whether they do party catering. A surprising amount will –- for this is where the really big bucks are (you know exactly how many you'll be feeding, and what they're going to eat). Always ask for references, and call a party giver who's used that caterer in the past. People are surprisingly forthright when the food has been disappointing.

I haven't had the opportunity to sample foods from the all of these caterers' menus, so I would be interested to hear any comments about these or other caterers you may have used.

Café Vert Catering
269a Archway Road, N6
0181 348 7666
Vegan options
Highgate's Café Vert also cater for events and, although their menu contains a couple of meat dishes, it is mainly vegetarian. The salads seem healthy and interesting, and the desserts mouthwatering, though options are not wildly adventurous. They are inexpensive (£5-10 per head for a choice of four to six dishes), and prices are inclusive of "quality disposable plates and cutlery" (which may be upsetting to the ecologists amongst us).

Café Pushka
16c Market Row, Brixton SW9
0171 738 6161
A friendly, unpretentious and decent little café that does outside catering. Your food should be good value for money if their café meals are anything to go by.

Catering Imaginaire
18 Belmont Court, Belmont Hill, St. Albans,
Herts,. AL1 1RB
01272 837643
Vegan options
Ros Masselin is a one woman vegetarian catering industry. Not only does she run the successful "Cuisine Imaginaire School for Green Cooks" (see page 82), and produces ready made veggie freezer meals, but she caters for many prestigious events in London. Options range from simple cocktail party or finger buffet menus, through to sit-down three course meals and dinner parties. The food has an international feel – couscous, guacamole, pesto – and Ros is very keen on the imaginative use of nuts and pulses. Her Wild Mushroom Strudel served with mushroom and brandy sauce is an inspired choice for a wedding dinner menu.

Green Door
18 Ashwin Street, Dalston, E8
0171 249 6793
Vegan options
Green Door offer a full catering service, with vegan and gluten free food, either at your venue, or deep in the heart of Dalston at the Green Door. The café can be privately hired for evenings or at weekends.

Green Fitz: Elite Meat-free catering

PO Box 11323
London N1 0QP
0171 637 0094/0956 463913
Vegan options

Green Fitz, named after Executive Chef Mark Fitzpatrick, was launched on World Vegetarian Day 1996, with the avowed intent of "declaring all out war on the omelette and the nut roast". They offer an international array of choices, with unusual and exotic spicing (Coconut curry or Milanese risotto with saffron for instance). Their textures are lighter and fruitier than one normally expects from vegetarian cooking.

Heather's Catering Service

190 Trundleys Road, Deptford, SE8
0181 691 6665
Vegan options

Heather's is one of London's best restaurants of any kind and, luckily for veggie party givers, they've decided to start an outside catering business. Heather's offer "anything from a simple platefull to an exotic buffet – with or without staff to assist in setting up, serving and clearing away". The food is almost certain to be wonderful, and the staff are invariably charming.

Kitchens of Resistance

42 Priory Road
London N8 7EX
0181 341 9610

Kitchens of Resistance are the people behind the little Planet Y café at the Crouch End YMCA, and were very helpful and generous in giving me several contacts for this book. They cater at private functions, at festivals and open air events, and offer a menu with a slightly Middle Eastern/ Mediterranean feel. They can also supply flowers, music, lighting, transport and security, and are among the most prompt and professional vegetarian caterers I have spoken to.

More Food For Thought

31 Neal Street, Covent Garden, WC2H 9PR
0171 836 9072
Vegan options

Food for Thought, having built an excellent reputation on the back of their packed Neal Street dining room, have now branched out into the world of corporate and event catering. Their menus are well laid out, making vegan and wheat free options quite clear, and have a good blend of internationally flavoured soups, hotpots, bakes and salads. The soups in particular stand out – carrot and tahini, cauliflower coconut and lime, lemon dahl – they sound and taste delicious (but I do wonder how easy it is to wolf them down at swish corporate lunches, mobile phone in one hand and press pack in the other).

Sharett

Unit A3, Connaught Business Centre, Hyde Estate Road, NW9 6JP
0181 200 1400

Neal Sharpe and Ruth Synett founded Sharett in 1991, and offer a one stop shop for event catering. Flowers, music, toast master, printing, wine, linen and glasses can all be arranged by them. They are a kosher caterers, with their own Supervised milk and meat kitchens in North London, so you can be sure that your vegetarian foods will not have been anywhere near animal flesh. Their staff are utterly professional, and their cocktail or buffet foods are imaginative and delicious – the mini latkes are moreish, as are the parsley fritters and cheese sambusak. I've worked with Neal and Ruth many times, and they've never let me (or their customers) down.

EXTRAS

OTHER SERVICES

DELIVERY SERVICE

Ivory Arch Tandoori

80-82 Walworth Road, Elephant & Castle SE1
0171 703 0182

Residents of central South London (SE1 and SE11) may not have many pleasures in life, but having one of the few vegetarian delivery servcies is one. The friendly staff from the Ivory Arch are normally banging the door down with your food within forty minutes, though they have a knack for getting lost (despite the fact that we live less than three streets away). Three set meals (£22 for two persons), ten main dishes, and a dozen starters and side dishes - it may not be much, but it's a start. Most of these are meat free versions of Punjabi favourites you'll find on many local curry house menus. But the fact that you can have it on your plate without having to brave the elements makes it all the more appreciated

CHARTERED ACCOUNTANTS

DRAKE & CO.

01932 562676

Ray and Shirley Drake are an imaginative and entrepreneurial husband and wife team of chartered accountants. They are also both vegetarian and vege friendly. They offer audit, accountancy and tax consultancy services, and are based just outside London in Chertsey.

COOKERY CLASSES

La Cuisine Imaginaire

18 Belmont Court, Belmont Hill, St. Albans, Herts. AL1 1RB
01272 837643

Ros Masselin's classes are now in their sixth year, and she continues to present one- four- and five-day courses for beginners or those with more experience. Offered at her schools in either St. Albans or London, all courses give students an opportunity to taste the food, and as the maximum class size is six, tuition is highly personal. Although many of the courses concentrate on styles and flavours of cooking, I was particularly interested to see Ros offering a programme in Dairy and Gluten-free cuisine. Prices start at £35.00 for a half day course.

Ursula Ferrigno

c/o Breakthrough Management
50 Turrene Close
London SW18 1JW
0181 870 8525

Anglo-Italian Ursula is a whirlwind of energy, whose passion for Italian and vegetarian food has made her a star of radio and television, and has pushed her onto her third book in as many years (see bibliography). She was principal tutor for the Vegetarian Society, runs six or seven courses a year at Books For Cooks (0171 221 1992), where her Sunday workshops are into their third term, and also teaches at Hansen's in the Fulham Road. She also teaches in Italy (call Nigel Haughton of La Cuccina Italiana 0181 743 4162). When I spoke to her she was breathlessly packing for a six week cookery cruise around the shores of Italy. It's so hard to keep up with Ursula that it's worth giving her a call to find out about future courses.

Ursula Ferrigno

MAGAZINES

BBC Vegetarian Good Food

Like vegetarian restaurants, magazines devoted to meat-free eating come and go at an alarming rate. The magazine market is, in any case, at saturation point, and few new titles manage to survive the three issue test. BBC Vegetarian Good Food is one that has, probably due to the financial clout of its parent organisation. It's a glossy monthly "bursting with flavour, health and vitality", is well designed and has those brief, visual pieces that seem to be fashionable in magazines right now. It's easily digestible, with matter of fact advice and exciting recipes, but somewhat thin on features and geared towards consumerism and shopping.

Most of the campaigning groups and vegetarian organisations listed in the book will also publish newsletters and magazines, each giving their own slant on meat-free living, and therefore more detailed in particular areas than BBC Vegetarian Good Food.

It's worth subscribing to at least two or three of these publications if you want to keep up with new restaurants, nutritional advice, and to find out what the larger chains are really up to.

VEGETARIAN GROUPS

Vegetarian Society

Parkdale
Dunham
Altrincham
Cheshire WA14 4QG
0161 928 0793

The Vegetarian Society estimate that there are now around four million vegetarians living in the UK. Compare this with only 100 000 in 1945 and one can appreciate a considerable shift in attitudes to meat eating. The Vegetarian Society produce a huge range of helpful books, magazines and leaflets for veggies, and is particularly useful for those considering the switch from an omnivorous lifestyle. They also run cookery courses and are the driving force behind National Vegetarian Week every year. A laudable organisation and one that provided me with many useful and interesting statistics for the book – did you know for instance that 16% of Londoners agree that vegetarians are more attractive than meat-eaters? Tell it like it is vege-dudes!

Vegan Society

7 Battle Road
St. Leonards-on-Sea
East Sussex TN37 7AA
01424 427393

A campaigning organisation that produces The Vegan magazine, and a host of useful books and pamphlets on issues around animal rights, and animal free lifestyles. More politicised than the Vegetarian Society, for obvious reasons but, I suspect, with wider grass roots support and a good network of local contacts. Membership is an ideal way of meeting like-minded friends.

Contact Centre (MV)
BCM Cuddle
London WC1V 6XX
Established over 16 years ago, the Contact Centre caters exclusively for vegetarians and vegans who wish to meet a partner. Life membership fees are extremely reasonable, and membership entitles you to order lists of contacts at a minimal extra cost. Contact Centre helps members make friends both in the UK and abroad (in countries as far apart as Argentina, Japan, and Nigeria). Contact Centre's Henk tells me that they "enjoy operating this service and we do not make profits".

Gay Vegetarians and Vegans
BM Box 5700
London WC1N 3XX
0181 470 1873
A friendly and informal group for lesbians, gay men and bisexual people which has been out and running since 1979. They meet once a month in East London and all are welcome, even those who have yet to decide whether they want to become veggies. They hope to launch a magazine this year, the wonderfully named 'Green Queen', for which they welcome letters, articles, news, fiction and poetry.

Jewish Vegetarian Society
Bet Teva
853/855 Finchley Road
London NW11 8LX
0181 455 0692
Part of an international movement committed to making known the teachings of Judaism on vegetarianism. The Jewish Vegetarian Society was established in 1964 and now has branches in over 20 countries. It seeks to remind Jews (and non-Jews) of God's laws on diet, which prohibit cruelty to animals. They are involved in political action, and have campaigned successfully in South Africa and Portugal (and stopped the introduction of bullfighting into Israel). They also organise conferences.

London Vegetarian Information Centre
c/o James Milton
19 Newlands Quay
London E1 9QZ
0171 702 3495
Jim says that the "Information Centre is the Vegetarian Society's smallest group. I aim to provide information to those visiting London (i.e. where to stay or eat) and to promote vegetarianism. I give talks to schools and other interested groups (for which there is no charge other than travelling expenses), and arrange social events."

London Vegans
7 Deansbrook Road
Edgware
Middx HA8 9BE
0181 746 2303
The organisation produces the useful London Vegan Diary, keeping its members abreast of veggie and vegan goings on in London. These include restaurant visits, walks, fundraising events and talks, and it seems to be a pretty well organised social network.

Vegetarian Matchmakers
Westside Chambers
13 Weston Park
London N8 9SY
0181 348 5229
Vegetarian Matchmakers offer a discreet service for vegetarians, vegans and aspiring veggies who want to meet soulmates. The organisation covers the whole of the UK and Ireland, and offers varying lengths of membership. Membership entitles you to attend social gatherings, and details of every member who may suit from a list which is constantly updated (in case Cupid's arrow doesn't twang immediately). It's approved by the Vegetarian Society which should give reassurance to those too shy or cautious to part with their money or reserve.

EXTRAS

All Walks Vegetarian Walkers

c/o Richard Cohen
110 Mildenhall Road
London E5 0RZ
0181 985 3892

All Walks began around ten years ago when the founders became fed up with being the butt of omnivorous walkers' jokes. They are a small and friendly group of individuals who do most of their walking on the South and North Downs. Although members are mostly from London, they do have one or two from as far afield as Winchester and Southampton. They meet for a trek on the first Sunday of every month, and membership costs £8/£5 concessions. Stroll on.

Vegetarian Wine Club

108 New Bond Street
London W1Y 9AA
No details were available at the time of going to press.

Young Indian Vegetarians

c/o Nitin Mehta
226 London Road
West Croydon
Surrey CR0 2TF
0181 681 8884

Young Indian Vegetarians are committed to improving animal rights and promoting 'Ahimsa' (respect for all living creatures), both in the UK and abroad. They are responsible for many vegetarian social events for Young Indians (though all are welcome at events like their Annual Hyde Park Vegetarian Picnic), but their newsletter also keeps members and supporters abreast of vegetarian and animal rights struggles around the world. Their September 1995 newsletter contained information on animal rights campaigns in France, Kenya, Mauritius and, of course, India.

Young Indian Vegetarians are also involved in the award of the Mahavir Medal, which is conferred on those who have worked tirelessly to end cruelty to animals and promote animal rights and vegetarianism. Their work in this country can best be summed up in Mahatma Gandhi's words " The moral progress of a nation should be judged by the way it treats its animals".

CAMPAIGNS

Living Without Cruelty Campaign

Animal Aid
The Old Chapel
Bradford Street
Tonbridge
Kent TN19 1AW

Living Without Cruelty sell their own range of cruelty free cosmetics, and send out information packs which point out alternatives to animal abuse.

Animal Liberation Front Supporters

BCM Box 1160 London WC1N 3XX

The ALF itself is illegal, but the supporters' group campaigns to set the record straight on animal rights protesters, vilified by the popular press, but who have a policy of not endangering animal or human life.

British Union for the Abolition of Vivisection

16a Crane Grove
London N7 8LB

Compassion in World Farming

Charles House
5a Charles Street, Petersfield
Hants. GU32

Set in the heart of the agricultural world, CIWF were behind the organisation of many of 1995's protests against the export of live calves. They know exactly what they're talking about as many of their members are farmers and country people. Members are currently braving the weather outside the Ministry of Agriculture Fisheries and Food in Whitehall – a vigil against the export trade they've sworn to carry on until the bloody business is stopped.

London Boots Action Group
c/o Alara
58 Seven Sisters Road
London N7 6AA
An organisation which campaigns against animal testing by picketing and leafleting Boots stores.

McLibel Support Campaign
c/o Greenpeace (London)
5 Caledonian Road
London N1 9DX
McDonalds are spending tens of thousands in court fees to prosecute two animal rights campaigners who leafleted their outlets, arguing that the information they handed out was libellous. The court case has become one of the longest running libel cases this century, and the McLibel campaign raises money for their defence.

National Anti-Vivisection Society
261 Goldhawk Road
London W12

National Society Against Factory Farming
91 Mercator Road
London SE13 5GH

People for the Ethical Treatment of Animals
PO Box 3169
London NW6 2QF

The Vegetarian Charity
14 Winters Lane
Ottery St. Mary
Devon EX1 1AR
Raises money to assist needy young vegetarians, and runs campaigns for young people promoting the benefits of a vegetarian lifestyle.

THE VEGETARIAN INTERNET

Only time will tell how useful a tool the internet is. Criticism currently revolves around the time taken to access certain pages, the amount of memory required to download sound and image, and the poor quality of information. Much of it is either second-hand, out of date, unverifiable, or just plain uninteresting. For instance, there isn't a decent guide to London eating places of any sort, let alone to veggie restaurants. What there is is outdated, and there is no excuse for such neglect in the most malleable and changeable of information formats. It takes minutes to change a listing electronically while to do the same in this book would require another edition – an expensive and time consuming process. As an example of the pitfalls of the web, UKdirectory's list of Cybercafés in Britain is not only out of date, but fails to list addresses, telephone numbers, or even the city in which each café is located. Pretty useless, I'm sure you'll agree.

You'll also discover that new web pages frequently appear and old ones disappear. Use a search engine such as Altavista, which will at least give you a good directory of what is available at any given time. I won't give individual web-site addresses – any search should turn these up. A week long trawl unearthed fun pages, useful information and some contentious stuff that was thought provoking and provided a few laughs along the way.

'Celebrity Vegetarians' for instance is little more than a list of those greats in all walks of life who don't eat flesh. But it's a long list and could be quite useful in lobbying for political change, featuring as it does a list of MPs (mostly Labour it has to be said). Perhaps no surprise to find that Tony Benn is a veg-head, or the ferocious Tony Banks, but who would have thought that Piers Merchant (Con., Beckenham) was also meat-free? Page Three girls Rachel Garley, Kathy Lloyd and Gail McKenna are also vegetarian, as are DJs John Peel, Tony Blackburn and Dave Lee Travis. After this list you may wonder whether anyone who had genuinely achieved greatness had ever chewed the lentil but, rest assured, the world would have remained resolutely unshaken without us herbivores: William Blake, Leonardo da Vinci, Einstein, Luther, Milton, Plato, Schopenhauer, Shaw, Shelley, Socrates and Tolstoy – you know you're in good company.

The Vegetarian Society provide useful information on diet and ethics on the web. There are well researched and easily absorbed pages relating to dietary requirements and the functions and sources of iron and other minerals and vitamins, or the uses of cereals such as soya, giving meal plans and medical advice. Importantly, these are accompanied by short bibliographies, which will mean that you can check the references (something many web-pages fail to provide).

Another interesting page supplied by the Vegetarian Society was 'Vegetarian Housing Towards the 21st Century', a report on providing sheltered housing for elderly vegetarians. A charity was founded as long ago as 1962 to create such a resource, and homes are now in operation in Hastings, Huddersfield, Cambridge and Horsham. With successive governments being uncommitted to providing shelter for any of their electors, the lessons that vegetarians have learned in setting up their own co-operative social and business networks can offer many lessons to the wider world.

Extremely useful to vegetarians, vegans (and, I would suggest, meat-eaters ignorant of what they are swallowing), is Vegan Action's 'Most Frequently Asked Questions', a list of around fifty queries that should just about clear up any confusion you have about what to eat or wear. Starting with "What are good books for new vegans?", and going through the more obvious ("Why

Not Leather?", "Should I be worried about not getting enough protein on a vegan diet?"), you then come to the more fascinating ethical questions. "Is Breast-feeding Vegan?" ("Don't be silly, of course it is!") - "Is Oral Sex Vegan?" ("Oral sex is vegan ... even though it may involve putting flesh in your mouth, it shouldn't really involve any cruelty or exploitation, as said flesh is taken out again eventually and returned to its rightful owner"). There is also good stuff on feeding cats and dogs on vegan diets though, interestingly, there is no discussion on the ethics of actually keeping a cat or dog.

Also fascinating, though of a rather more scholarly timbre, is John Davis' 'Food in England since 1066 – A Vegetarian Evolution'. This is a series of four articles looking at animal and plant-based diets in England over the past millennium. The lists of foodstuffs on the mediaeval table can become a bit tiring, but Davis' thesis is that there has been a gradual improvement in the incidence of vegetarianism in the diet, despite evidence that variety in our diet is in a sadly impoverished state compared with that of our ancient ancestors.

If you don't have access to the internet, at home or at work, you may want to take yourself along to one of London's cybercafés, though food isn't a priority, and asking for the menu may cause some confusion. And for those that are not computer illiterate, or who can't be bothered, there are these things called libraries ...

Cyberia Café
39 Whitfield Street, W1P 5RE
0171 209 0983
Transport: Goodge Street LU

Café Internet
22-24 Buckingham Palace Road, SW1W 0QP
0171 233 5786
Transport: Victoria LU/BR

Cyberia Café

BIBLIOGRAPHY (with special thanks to Celia Brooks-Brown)

The British at Table 1940-1980 - Christopher Driver (Chatto & Windus)

Evergreen - Annie Bell (MacMillan)

The Flavour of California - Marlena Speiler

Food Lovers London - Jenny Linford (Metro)

Foods of the World (Time Life)

Good Cheap Eats in London 1995/6 (Harden's Guides)

The Good Curry Restaurant Guide - Pat Chapman (Curry Club)

The Good Food Guide 1995 - Ed. Jim Ainsworth (Which)

Good to Eat: Riddles of Food and Culture - Marvin Harris (Allen and Unwin)

The Greens Cookbook - Deborah Madison (Bantam Books)

Guide to Ethnic London - Ian McAuley (Immel)

The Inspired Vegetarian - Louise Pickford

Middle Eastern Vegetarian Cookery - David Scott (Rider)

New Food - Jill Dupleix (Mitchell Beazley)

Pizza, Pasta and Polenta - Ursula Ferrigno (Merehurst)

Real Fast Vegetarian Food - Ursula Ferrigno (Metro Books)

Sundays at Moosewood Restaurant: Ethnic and Regional Recipes from the Cooks at the Legendary Restaurant - Moosewood Collective (Fireside)

A Taste of London - Theodora Fitzgibbon (Pan)

Time Out Eating & Drinking Guide 1995 - Ed. Sarah Guy (Time Out)

Vatch's Thai Cookbook - Vatcharin Bhumichitr (Pavilion)

Verdura - Viana la Place (McMillan)

Virtually Vegetarian - Paul Gayler (Harper Collins)

Name	Nationality	Vegetarian (V) Meat & Vegetarian (M)	Area	Page No.
Taboon	Jewish	V	E1	23
Cherry Orchard	General	V	E2	23
Thai Garden	Thai	M	E2	23
Café Alba	General	M	E8	24
Green Door Wholefood Café	International	V	E8	24
Al's Diner	General	M	EC1	25
Axiom Café	General	V	EC1	25
Community Health Foundation Lunch Club	General	V	EC1	25
Cranks	General	V	EC1	26
Carnevale	Mediterranean	V	EC1	26
The Place Below	Mediterranean	V	EC2	26
Futures Take-away	General-snacks	V	EC3	26
Bennett and Luck	General	V	N1	28
Candid Café	General	M	N1	28
Charminar	Indian	V	N1	29
Indian Vegetarian Bhel-Poori House	Indian	V	N1	29
Pasha	Middle-Eastern	M	N1	29
Pizza Express	Italian	M	N1	30
Rye Wholefoods	General	V	N1	30

Name	Nationality	Vegetarian (V) Meat & Vegetarian (M)	Area	Page No.
Mahavir Sweet Mart	Indian-snacks	V	N2	30
Mandarin	Chinese	M	N2	30
Café Vert	General	V	N6	32
Jai Krishna	Indian	V	N4	32
Rani	Indian	V	N3	32
Planet Y	General	V	N8	33
World Café	Mediterranean	M	N8	33
Oshobasho Café	General	V	N10	34
Magpie & Stump	British	M	N16	34
Rasa	Indian	V	N16	34
Chutneys	Indian	V	NW1	35
Diwana	Indian	V	NW1	35
Ravi Shankar	Indian	V	NW1	35
St Marylebone Café	General	V	NW1	35
Manna	General	V	NW3	37
Vegetarian Cottage	Chinese	V	NW3	37
Geeta	Indian	M	NW6	38
Surya	Indian	V	NW6	38
Good Earth	International	V	NW7	38
Abeno	Japanese	M	NW9	38
Taboon Bakery	Jewish	V	NW11	39
Pizza Express	Italian	M	NW11 NW3	39

Name	Nationality	Vegetarian (V) Meat & Vegetarian (M)	Area	Page No.
Sabras	Indian	V	NW10	39
Imperial Tandoori	Indian	M	SE1	40
Ivory Arch Tandoori	Indian	V	SE1	40
Jumbleys	General	M	SE1	40
Pizza Express	Italian	M	SE1	40
Carrot Café	International	V	SE5	41
Heathers Café Bistro	General	V	SE8	41
Escaped	International	V	SE10	42
Oval Café	International	V	SE11	42
Mantanah	Thai	M	SE25	42
Institute of Contemporary Arts	Italian	V	SW1	43
The Lanesborough	International	V	SW1	43-44
Pizza on the Park	Italian	M	SW1	44
Wilkins	General	V	SW1	44
Woodlands	Indian	V	SW1	44
Wren at St James	General	V	SW1	44
Bah Humbug	General	V	SW2	44
Peter Peppers Mediterranean Café	Mediterranean	V	SW2	45
Good Earth	International	V	SW3	45
Kings Road Café	General	M	SW3	46

Name	Nationality	Vegetarian (V) Meat & Vegetarian (M)	Area	Page No.
Sydney Street Café	General	M	SW3	46
Eco	Italian	M	SW4	46
Balans West	International	M	SW5	46
Gardeners	International	V	SW6	47
Mamta	Indian	V	SW6	47
Windmill Wholefoods	General	V	SW6	47
Tea Room Des Artistes	International	V	SW8	47
Asmara	African	M	SW9	48
Café Pushka	General	V	SW9	48
The Jakaranda Garden	International	M	SW9	48
Pizza Express	Italian	M	SW10 SW11 SW14 SW15	48 50 50
Wholemeal Café	International	V	SW16	50
Kastoori	Indian	V	SW17	50
Milan	Indian	V	SW17	50
Sree Krishna	Indian	M	SW17	51
Tumbleweeds	International	V	SW17	51
Pizza Express	Italian	M	SW18	51
Good Earth	International	V	SW19	51
Pizza Express	Italian	M	SW19	51
Pierre Lapin	French	V	SW19	51
Balans	International	M	W1	52

Name	Nationality	Vegetarian (V) Meat & Vegetarian (M)	Area	Page No.
Cranks	General	V	W1	52
Govindas	Indian	V	W1	53
Kettners	Italian	M	W1	53
Mildred's	International	V	W1	53
Minara	Indian	V	W1	55
Pizza Express	Italian	M	W1	55
Pollo	Italian	M	W1	55
Presto	Italian	M	W1	55
Ragam	Italian	M	W1	56
Shilla	Korean	M	W1	56
The Veraswamy	Indian	M	W1	56
Woodlands	Indian	V	W1	56
Diwana	Indian	V	W2	56
Pizza Express	Italian	M	W2 W4 W5	56 57 57
The Gate	International	V	W6	57
Pizza Express	Italian	M	W8	57
Books for Cooks	International	M	W11	58
Leith's	Modern British	M	W11	58
MandolaCafé	African	M	W11	58
Pizza Express	Italian	M	W11 W11	58 58
Blah Blah Blah	International	V	W12	59
The Greenhouse	General	V	WC1	60

Name	Nationality	Vegetarian (V) Meat & Vegetarian (M)	Area	Page No.
Pizza Express	Italian	M	WC1	60
Wagamama	Japanese	M	WC1	60
Bunjies	General	V	WC2	62
Calabash	African	M	WC2	62
Cranks	General	V	WC2	62
First Out	General	V	WC2	62
Food for Thought	General	V	WC2	63
Gaby's Continental Bar	International	M	WC2	63
The Café	General	V	WC2	63
Neal's Yard Bakery & Tea Room	General	V	WC2	64
Vegetarian Cuisine	General	V	WC2	64
World Food Café	International	V	WC2	64
Paprika Vegetarian Restaurant	General	V	WC2	64
'A' Sweet	Indian-snacks	V	UB1	66
Balti Hut	Indian	V	HA2	66
Chetna's	Indian	V	HA9	67
Hockney's	General	V	CR0	67
Rajbhog	Indian	V	HA9	67
Rani	Indian	V	TW9	67
Woodlands	Indian	V	HA9	67

London's Top Ten Veggies

Heathers SE8 (p.41)
For the friendly service, relaxed atmosphere, and great food. Heathers is a restaurant where the staff obviously wholeheartedly believe in what they're doing, and that comes across in their food.

Lanesborough SW1 (p.43-44)
A luxurious treat in sumptuous surroundings. The food is heavenly too, and though by no means a budget choice, you deserve to treat yourself every once in a while.

Kastoori SW17 (p.50)
The influences of Western India and East Africa combine, making an excursion to Tooting a must.

Mahavir N2 (p.30)
The best samosas in London, and every chilli fanatic should experience their chilli flavoured potato chips.

Food for Thought WC2 (p.63)
Still one of London's best, and beating all competition in the Covent Garden area.

Gaby's WC2 (p.63)
Cheap, cheerful and chunky Middle-Eastern delights.

Books for Cooks W11 (p.58)
Never disappointing, though you'll inevitably have to queue for a table. Don't take too much money though – you'll spend it on books.

The Gate W6 (p.57)
It's been around a while now, despite rumours that it's not as good as it was. Never fear – it is!

Mantanah SE25 (p.42)
Spicy Thai treats in comfortable surroundings.

Gardners SW6 (p.47)
A new veggie restaurant, and though it's not quite as good as the reviews claim, it will be.

INDEX

ORDER FORM

Send your order and payment to:
METRO PUBLICATIONS
PO BOX 6336
LONDON
N1 6PY
Postage and packing free

Please send me
copy/ copies of

| 1 | 2 |

Veggie London by Craig John Wilson

I enclose payment of
(cheques made payable
to Metro Publications)

| 5.99 | 11.98 |

Please send me
copy/ copies of

| 1 | 2 |

Gay London by Graham Parker

I enclose payment of
(cheques made payable
to Metro Publications)

| 6.99 | 13.98 |

Please send me
copy/ copies of

| 1 | 2 |

Bargain Hunters' London

I enclose payment of
(cheques made payable
to Metro Publications)

| 5.99 | 11.98 |

Name : _____

Address : _____

_____

_____

Please keep me informed about
forthcoming publications.

ORDER FORM

Send your order and payment to:
METRO PUBLICATIONS
PO BOX 6336
LONDON
N1 6PY
Postage and packing free

Please send me
copy/ copies of

1	2

Food Lover's London by Jenny Linford

I enclose payment of
(cheques made payable
to Metro Publications)

5.99	11.98

Please send me
copy/ copies of

1	2

The London Market Guide

I enclose payment of
(cheques made payable
to Metro Publications)

3.99	7.98

Name : _____

Address : _____

_____

Please keep me informed about
forthcoming publications.

_____